AMERICAN
ARMORED
FIGHTING VEHICLES

GEORGE BRADFORD

STACKPOLE
BOOKS

Published by
STACKPOLE BOOKS
5067 Ritter Road
Mechanicsburg, PA 17055
www.stackpolebooks.com

Cover design by Wendy A. Reynolds

Printed in the United States of America

10 9 8 7 6 5 4 3 2 1

FIRST EDITION

Library of Congress Cataloging-in-Publication Data

Bradford, George.
   American armored fighting vehicles / George Bradford. — 1st ed.
      p. cm. — (World War II AFV Plans)
   Includes bibliographical references.
   ISBN-13: 978-0-8117-3340-3
   ISBN-10: 0-8117-3340-8
   1. Armored vehicles, Military—United States. 2. Tanks (Military science)—United States. I. Title.

   UG446.5.B682 2007
   623.7'475097309044—dc22
                                                      2006038952

Contents

Introduction

This second volume in this series of books on scale drawings of armored fighting vehicles of World War II is devoted to American military vehicles which were produced in the USA leading up to and during WWII. Many of these vehicles were either in use or in development from 1936 to 1945, and are shown here roughly in chronological order of appearance on the scene. However, there was much overlap in vehicle production, and this makes it somewhat difficult to establish a sequence which is totally perfect.

Therefore, if you are looking for armored vehicles used by United States forces before and during World War II, then you should be able to find many of them in this book. Some of the vehicles manufactured by the U.S. in WWII were used solely by Britain and her Commonwealth allies. However, since they were manufactured in the USA they are shown here as well.

Among the vehicles covered you will find some of the prototypes that never really saw action, plus some of the vehicles that were just too late to participate in the war. You will also find that we cover mainly armored fighting vehicles, but also with a few support vehicles that fought along side of them thrown in.

The ultimate purpose of this series of books is to try and present a sequence of World War II military vehicle plan view scale drawings all in one place. Most of these drawings display 4-view plans, but with some of the smaller vehicles we were able to show five or more views. Over the years, scale drawings of various armored vehicles have appeared in various publications, but never all in one place where they would be easy for the researcher or modeler to access them.

Armored vehicle drawings have always appeared in various scales in different magazines and books, but the more popular ones of late have boiled down to mainly 1:35, 1:48 and 1:72 in the armor modeling world. With this in mind we have tried to keep the drawings as large as possible with a preponderance of 1:35 scale drawings, supported by 1:48 scale where appropriate, and also for vehicles that are simply too big to fit on the page comfortably as 1:35 scale drawings.

You will also find a chart at the beginning of this book for reducing or enlarging any of these drawings to other popular scales. The quality and accuracy of modern photocopying should make it possible for you to achieve whatever final scale you require. However, in some cases where enlargement is required, you may only be able to squeeze one view onto letter size paper and may have to utilize 11" x 17" paper where available.

These drawings have been created using vector based drawing applications with line weights ranging from .25 point to 1 point, and thus should easily hold the finer detail when copying. The bulk of these drawings were done over a period of ten years and are currently among the most precise and accurate AFV drawings available. You will also notice a variance in the drawings as the art style changes slightly over the years, but eventually supports shading in the majority of the later works.

SCALE CONVERSIONS

REDUCING

1:35 to 1:48 Scale = 73%

1:35 to 1:76 Scale = 46%

1:35 to 1:72 Scale = 49%

1:35 to 1:87 Scale = 41%

1:48 to 1/76 Scale = 63%

1:48 to 1:72 Scale = 66%

1:48 to 1:87 Scale = 55%

1:72 to 1:76 Scale = 95%

ENLARGING

1:35 to 1:32 Scale = 109%

1:35 to 1:16 Scale = 218%

1:48 to 1:35 Scale = 138%

1:48 to 1:32 Scale = 150%

1:48 to 1:16 Scale = 300%

1:72 to 1:35 Scale = 207%

1:72 to 1:48 Scale = 150%

1:72 to 1:16 Scale = 450%

Combat Car, M1

(c. 1937)

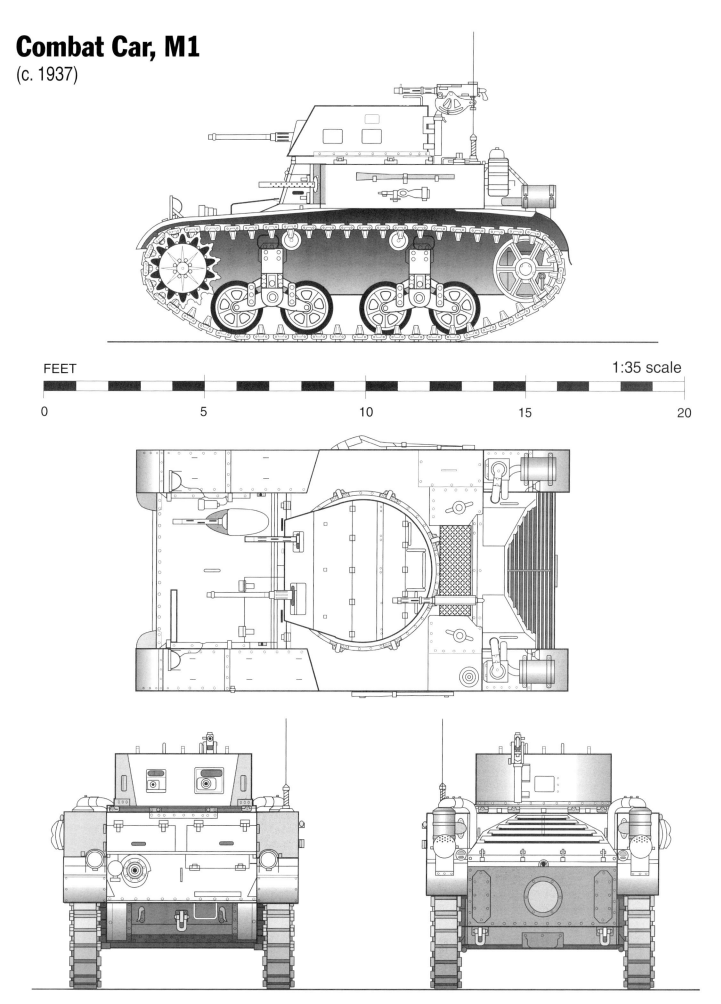

FEET

1:35 scale

0   5   10   15   20

A late model M1 Combat Car with the angular flat sided turret, seen during tests
carried out at Fort Knox, Kentucky by the 7th Cavalry Brigade in May 1938.

Cpt. Henry Cabot Lodge, Senator from Massachusetts participates in a light tank drill at Fort Knox, July 28, 1940.
This is the later M1A1 Combat Car, with elongated suspension.

Combat Car M2
(Light Tank M1A1)

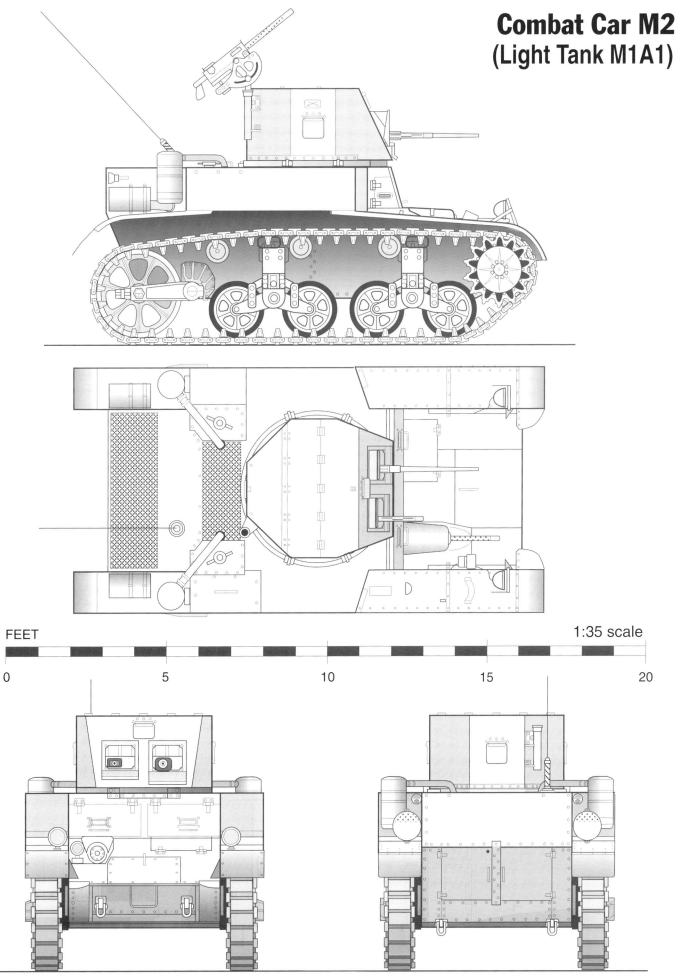

FEET

1:35 scale

0   5   10   15   20

M1 Armored Car
(T4 Standardized)

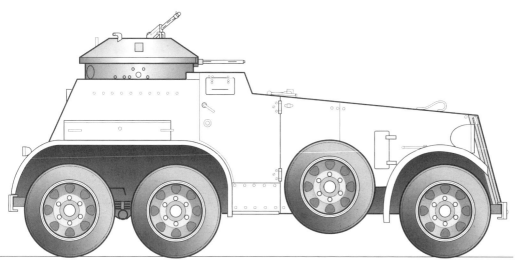

In 1932 the U.S. Armored Car T4 was a pace setter for its time, since rather than being based on an existing commercial 2-wheel drive chassis, it was designed as a 6x4 high speed 4-wheel drive vehicle. It was also innovative in that the wheels and suspension were attached directly to the hull. The spindles of the spare tires either side were free to revolve, and were placed low enough to aid in traversing low obstacles.

Produced by the James Cunningham Company, it was powered by their 133 hp V8 engine. They were still in use with the 7th Cavalry Brigade from Ft. Knox in a massed exercise in N.Y. state in the summer of 1939.

FEET

1:35 scale

0   5   10   15   20

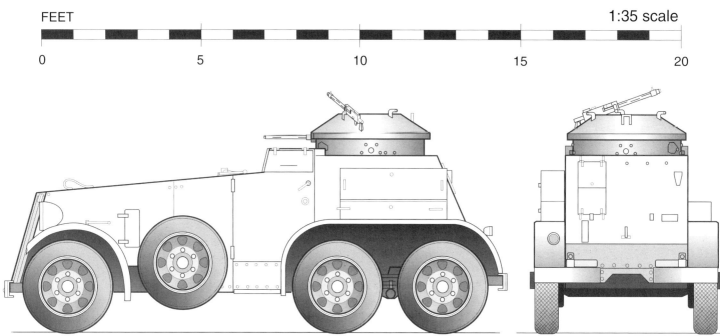

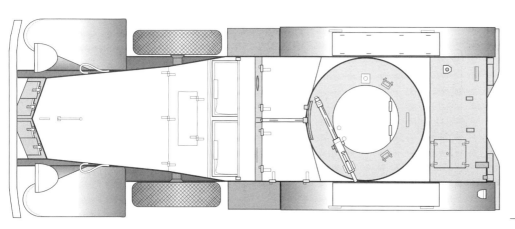

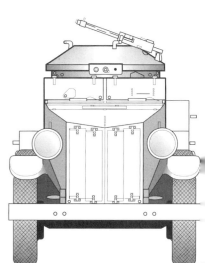

Light Tank, M2A2

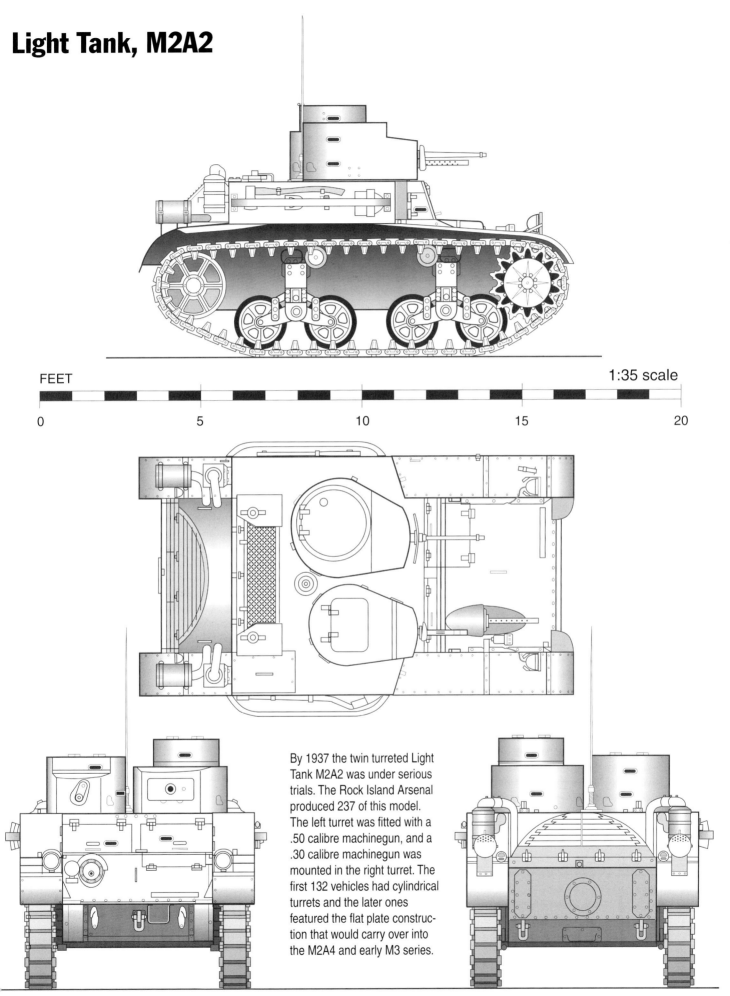

FEET

1:35 scale

0   5   10   15   20

By 1937 the twin turreted Light Tank M2A2 was under serious trials. The Rock Island Arsenal produced 237 of this model. The left turret was fitted with a .50 calibre machinegun, and a .30 calibre machinegun was mounted in the right turret. The first 132 vehicles had cylindrical turrets and the later ones featured the flat plate construction that would carry over into the M2A4 and early M3 series.

Light Tank, M2A3

(c. 1938)

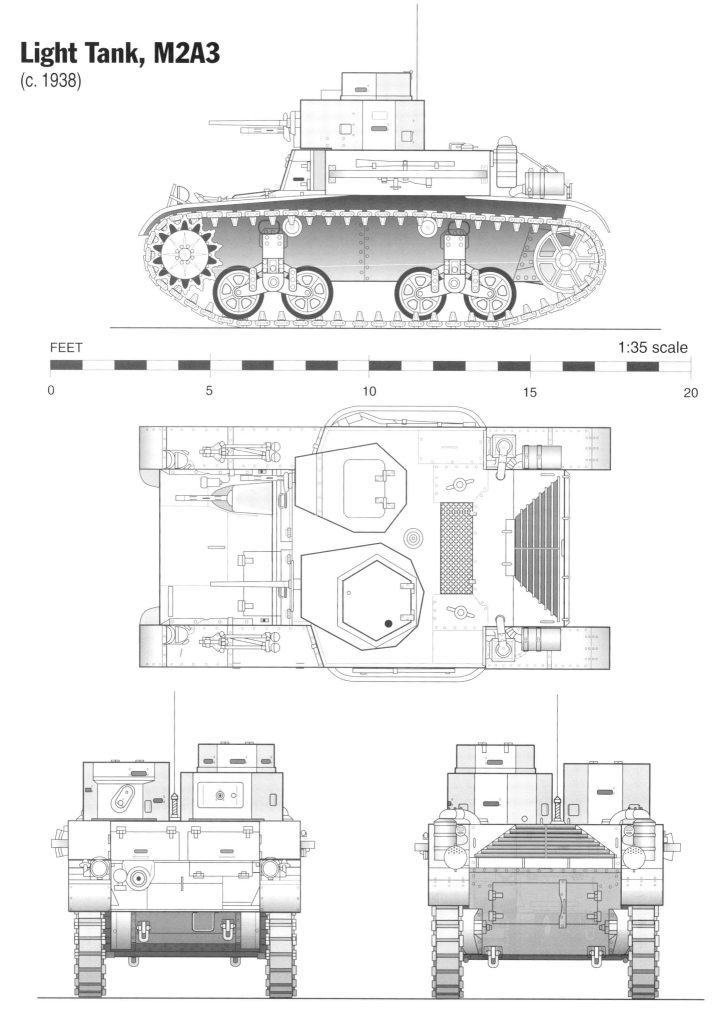

FEET

1:35 scale

0   5   10   15   20

Light Tank, M2A4

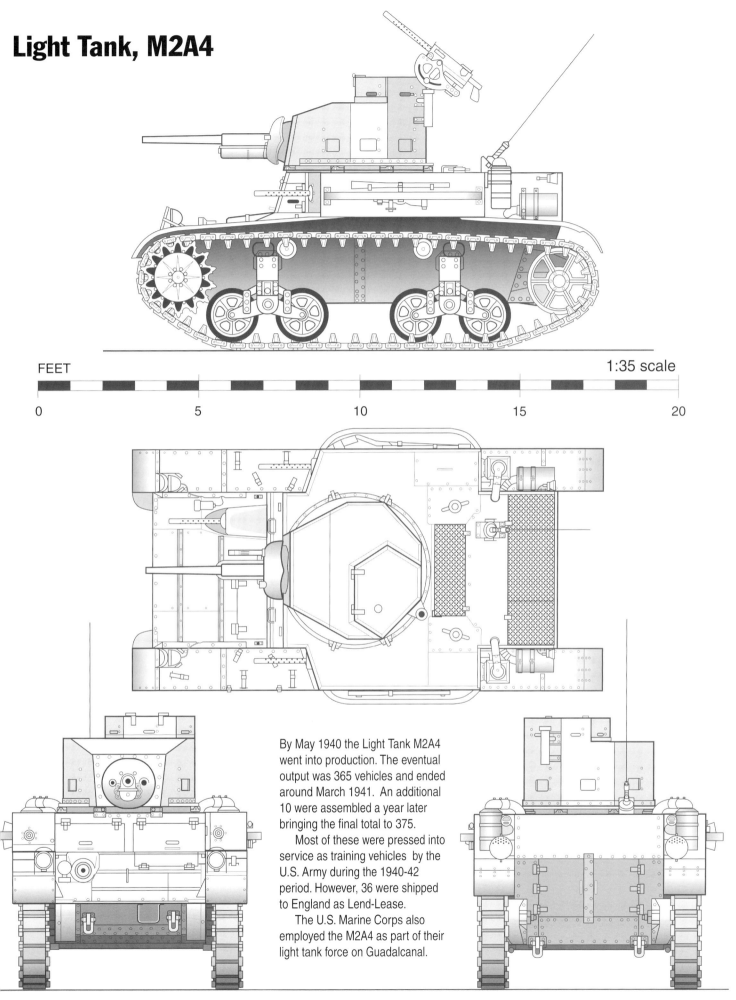

FEET

1:35 scale

0   5   10   15   20

By May 1940 the Light Tank M2A4 went into production. The eventual output was 365 vehicles and ended around March 1941. An additional 10 were assembled a year later bringing the final total to 375.

Most of these were pressed into service as training vehicles by the U.S. Army during the 1940-42 period. However, 36 were shipped to England as Lend-Lease.

The U.S. Marine Corps also employed the M2A4 as part of their light tank force on Guadalcanal.

Two views of M2A4 Light Tanks being delivered to Fort Ord, California in 1941. Their main identifying features are the wide gap between the front and rear bogey, and the elevated rear idler. The construction in the background is the new barracks and recreation center just going up.

M3A1 White Scout Car

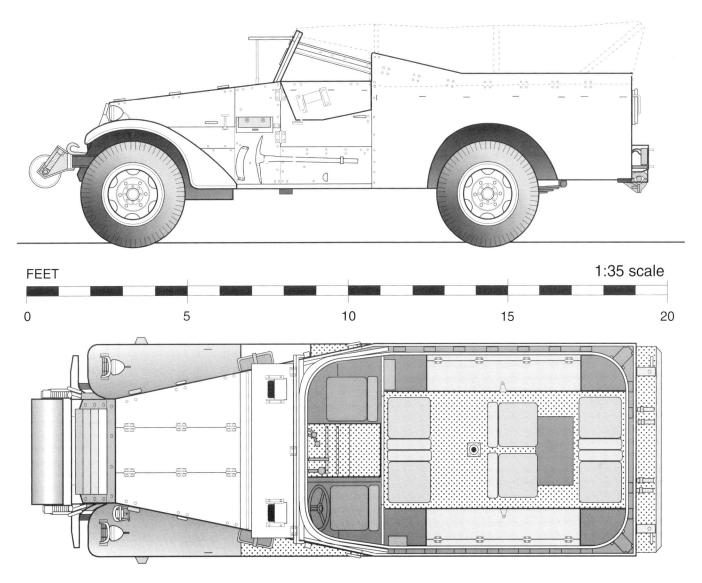

FEET

1:35 scale

0　　　　　　　5　　　　　　　10　　　　　　　15　　　　　　　20

Interior dashboard detail.

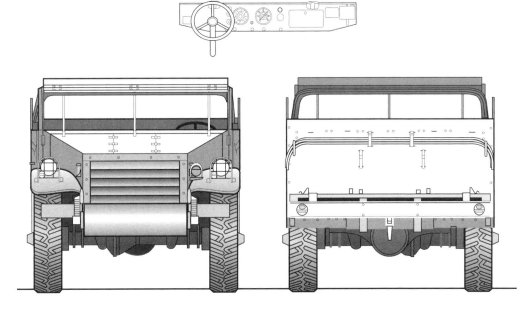

All during World War Two the White Motor Company was producing the M3A1 Scout Cars. They were the pre-war M3 Scout Car but with a wider hull and the sprung roller on the front. A total of 20,856 were built during the war to serve as anything from armored personnel carriers, command vehicles or ambulances. They came with a removeable tarpaulin top, sometimes referred to as a "tilt".

The M3A1 Scout Cars were supplied to many countries during the war, including Russia and Canada, and also soldiered on in lesser nations well after WW2.

Medium Tank, M2A1

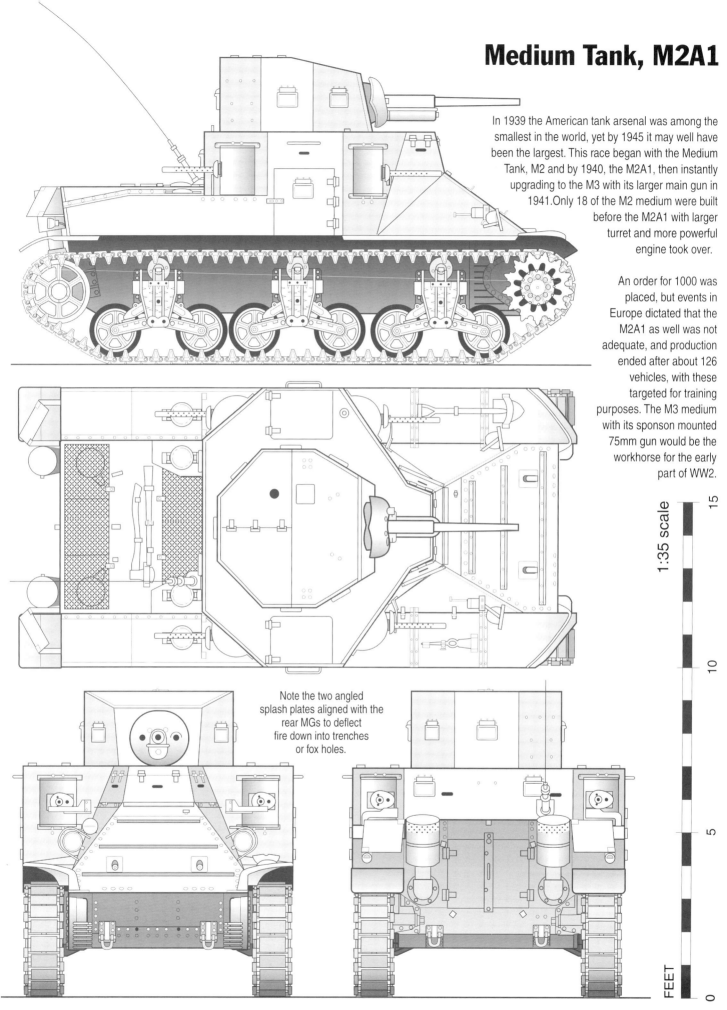

In 1939 the American tank arsenal was among the smallest in the world, yet by 1945 it may well have been the largest. This race began with the Medium Tank, M2 and by 1940, the M2A1, then instantly upgrading to the M3 with its larger main gun in 1941.Only 18 of the M2 medium were built before the M2A1 with larger turret and more powerful engine took over.

An order for 1000 was placed, but events in Europe dictated that the M2A1 as well was not adequate, and production ended after about 126 vehicles, with these targeted for training purposes. The M3 medium with its sponson mounted 75mm gun would be the workhorse for the early part of WW2.

Note the two angled splash plates aligned with the rear MGs to deflect fire down into trenches or fox holes.

1:35 scale

15

10

5

FEET

0

M2 Half-track Car

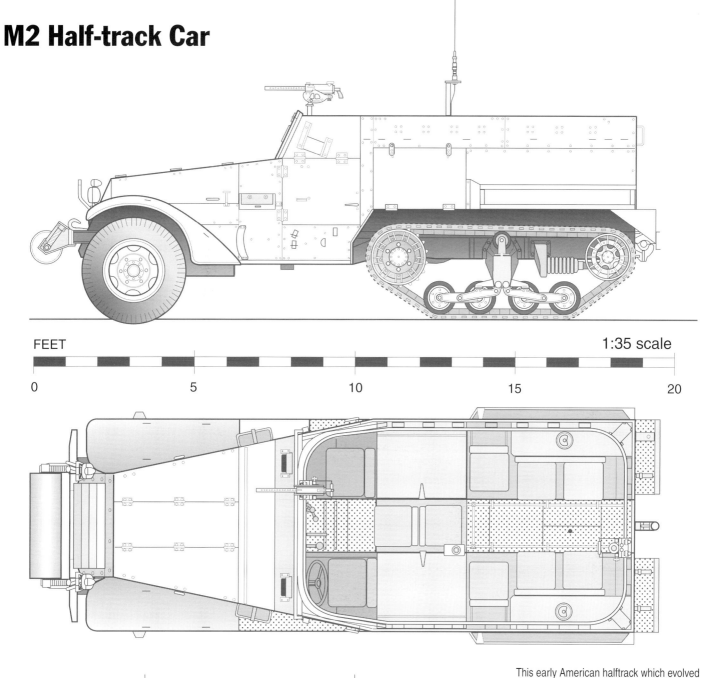

FEET   1:35 scale

0   5   10   15   20

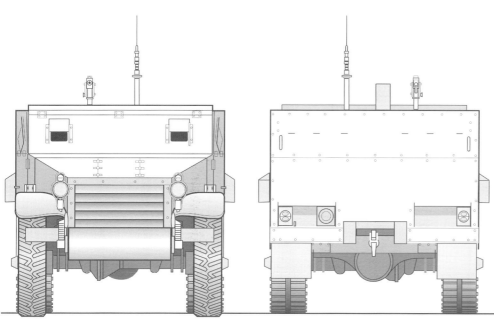

This early American halftrack which evolved from the T14, was produced from early 1941 to mid-1943. Powered by a White 160AX engine it proved relatively simple to produce and a total of 11,415 came off the line before it was finally phased out in favour of later models. It was built by both White and Autocar facilities. A characteristic feature of the M2 was the skate rail which ran all the way around its shorter open body, and the large storage bins dividing the driving compartment from the rear troop seating area. The M2 also features shorter anti-tank mine racks along each side, aft of the large storage bin side-access doors.

The main problem found with the M2 layout was the lack of rear access caused by the continuous skate rail traversing the entire rim of the interior. In addition to the skate rail there was also a pedestal mount for the MG between the storage boxes.

T16 Half-track Car
Test Vehicle built by Autocar

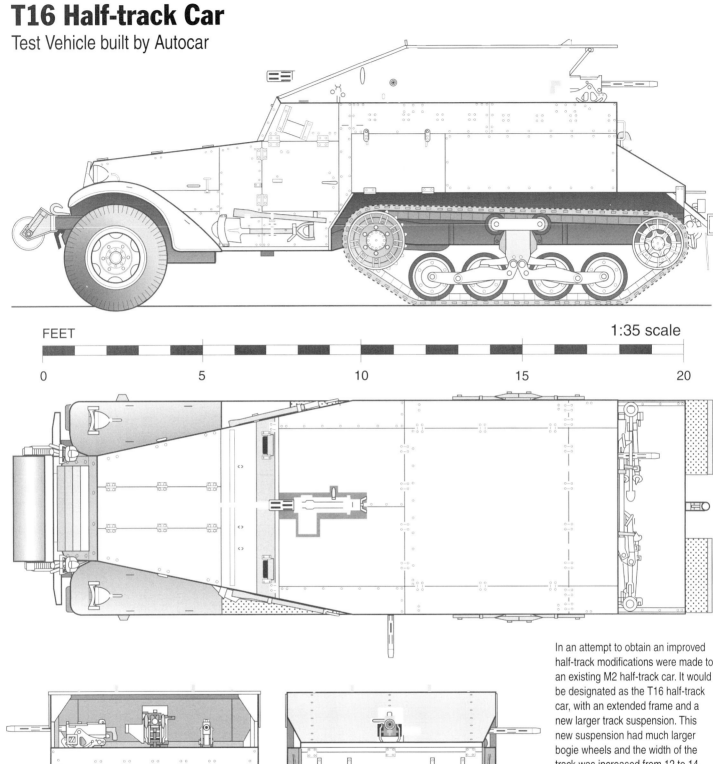

FEET

1:35 scale

0   5   10   15   20

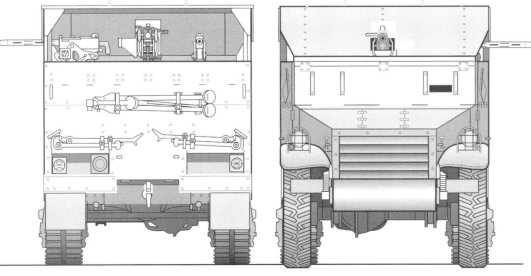

In an attempt to obtain an improved half-track modifications were made to an existing M2 half-track car. It would be designated as the T16 half-track car, with an extended frame and a new larger track suspension. This new suspension had much larger bogie wheels and the width of the track was increased from 12 to 14 inches wide with a longer ground contact area as well. A unique feature of the T16 test vehicle was the addition of a 1/4" thick folding armor plate roof. The center portion of the frontal area could be flipped back for better visibility while on the move. However, in the end it was deemed that this armor roof was not practical, and the overall performance of the test vehicle was unsatisfactory. Further work on the T16 program was stopped in early 1942.

Marmon-Herrington
CTMS-1TB1

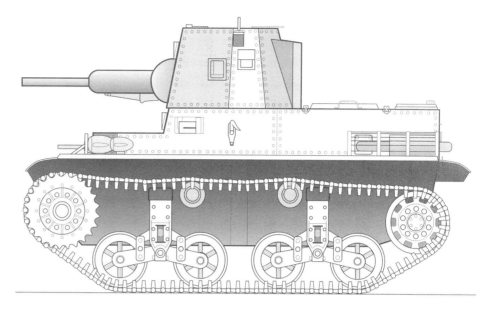

Among the more obscure American tanks is the series of vehicles produced by the Marmon-Herrington Company. The majority of their vehicles were built for export, most notably for Persia, China and The Netherlands.

Included in a 600 tank deal with The Netherlands in 1941 was their heavier CTMS 1TB1 3-man light tank, commonly referred to as the "Dutch Three Man Tank". However, the Japanese swept through the Dutch East Indies by the time the first deliveries had arrived, and none of the CTMS tanks were shipped.

With America now drawn into WW2 the U.S. government took control of all war material production and the U.S. Army tested the M-H series of tanks, but deemed them inadequate. However, some were used for training purposes and the model CTLS-4TAC was actually designated as Light Tank T16 and saw patrol duty in Alaska. The rejected CTMS light tanks were eventually supplied to Ecuador, Dutch Guyana, Cuba, Mexico, and Guatemala.

The CTMS mounted an automatic 37mm cannon with coaxial & bow .30 cal MG, and weighed in at about 12.5 tons. The two protrusions on the rear of the turret act as counterweights for the main armament. Note that the plates are not riveted, but rather use low profile slot-head bolts.

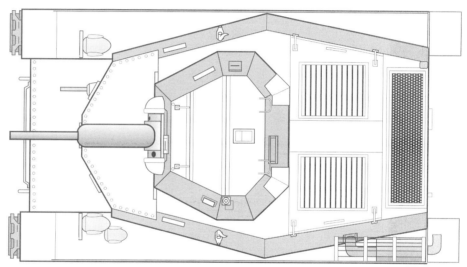

FEET

1:35 scale

0   5   10   15   20

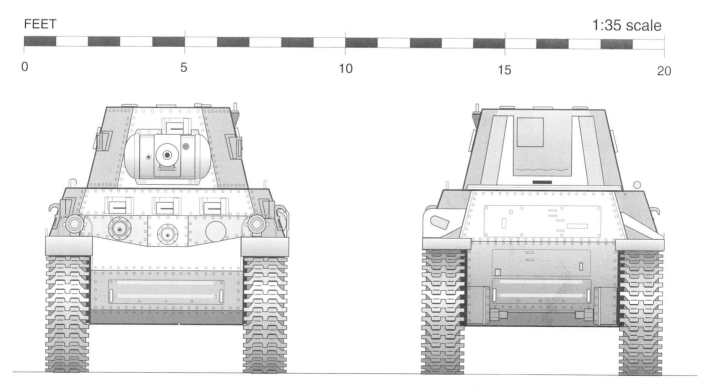

Marmon-Herrington
MTLS-1GI4 4-man (Virgie)

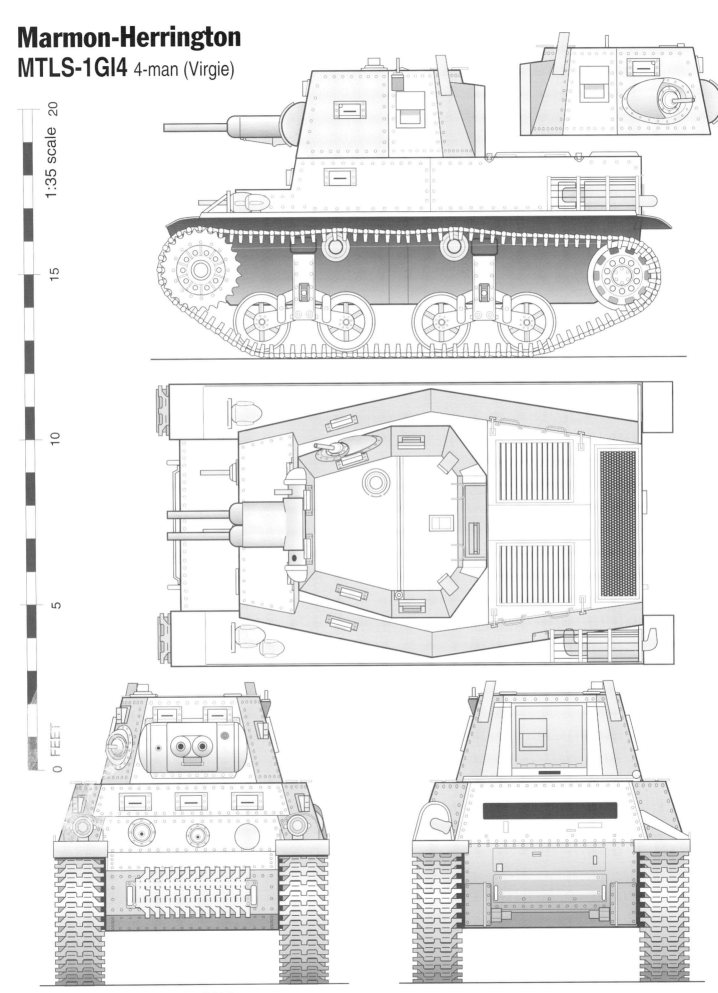

1:35 scale

20

15

10

5

0 FEET

M3 75mm Gun Motor Carriage

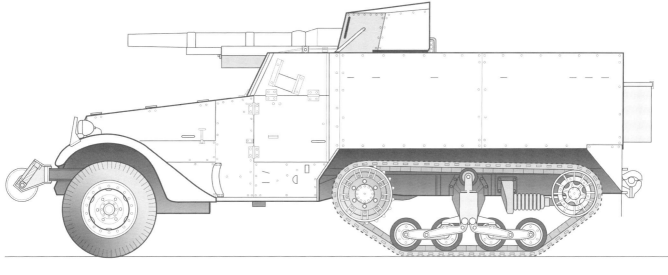

FEET

1:35 scale

0   5   10   15   20

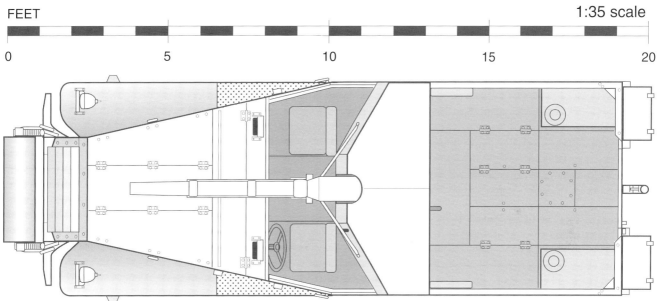

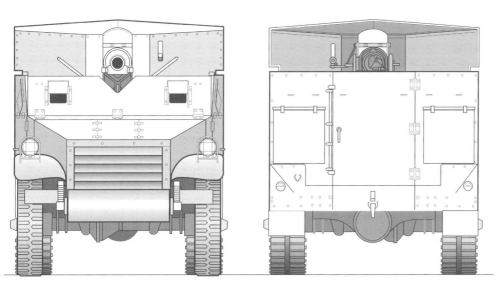

Based on the production model gun motor carriage T12 the 75mm GMC M3 went into production by November 1941 in an attempt to quickly field an expedient tank destroyer. The GMC T12 was fitted with a simple gun shield and the old pre-WWI M1897A4 "French 75" mainly because they were readily available. The gun had been slightly modernized, but from the start this vehicle was considered only as a stop-gap until a more suitable tank destroyer could be fielded.The contract was given to the Autocar Company of Ardmore, PA and by the end of 1941 a total of 86 were delivered to the Army. Production in 1942 totalled 1,350, and 766 by April 1943, when production ceased. The final batch used up most of the older M2A2 carriages, since the M2A3 stock had run out, and these were referred to as the 75mm GMC M3A1. Their debut of action in Tunisia was far from impressive, but finally when employed properly they did manage to hold their own, and were eventually relegated to more of a mobile infantry support weapon than a true tank destroyer. It carried a crew of five.

A view of the T12 very early M3 GMC when the 75mm gun mount still retained the original field gun shield, rather than the later box shaped shield. Seen here at Fort Hood, Texas in 1941.

An early Light Tank M3 showing the new trailing idler suspension, round air cleaners and riveted turret assembly. The sponson MGs shown here were soon to be plated over.

M3 Light Tank
Light Tank M3 (early production)

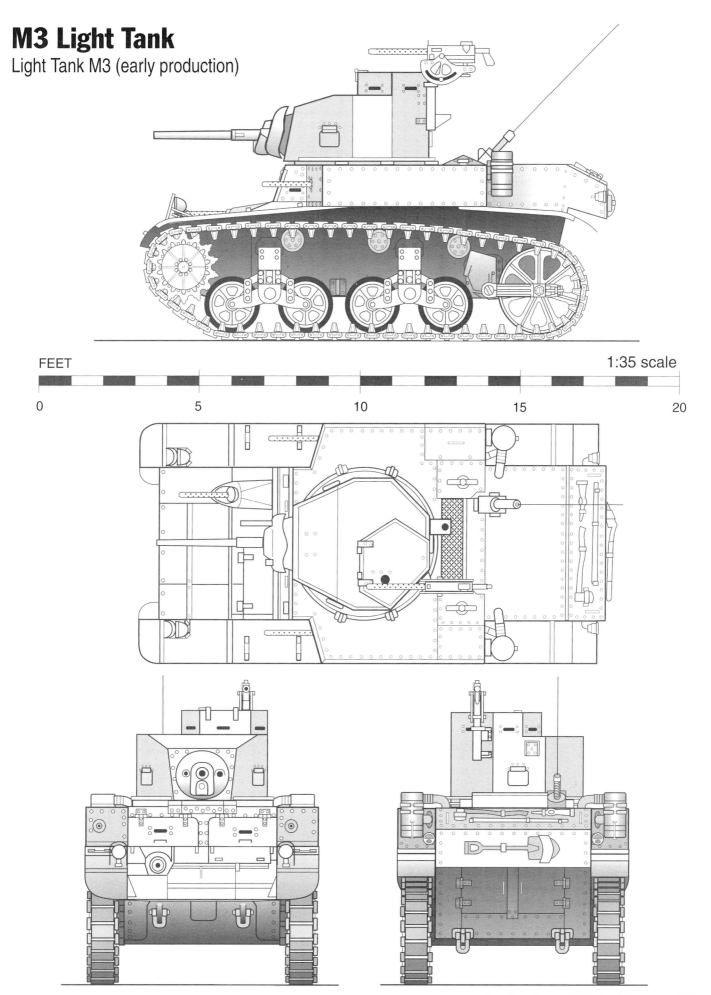

FEET

1:35 scale

0   5   10   15   20

M3 'Lee " Medium Tank
An early M3 medium still fitted with the short 75mm gun M2

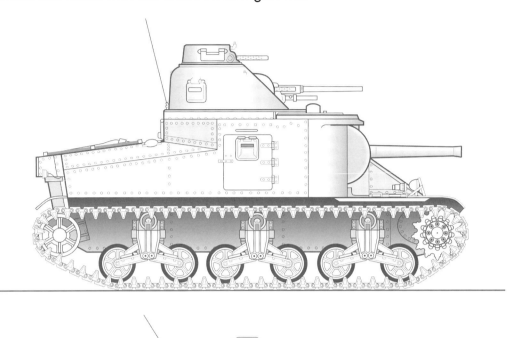

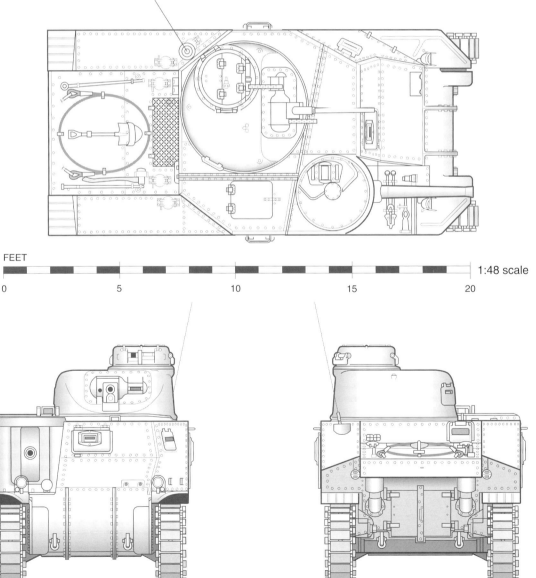

FEET

1:48 scale

0   5   10   15   20

A nice high angle view of the early M3 Lee Medium Tank undergoing performance tests.

Tank, M4A1

Initial production

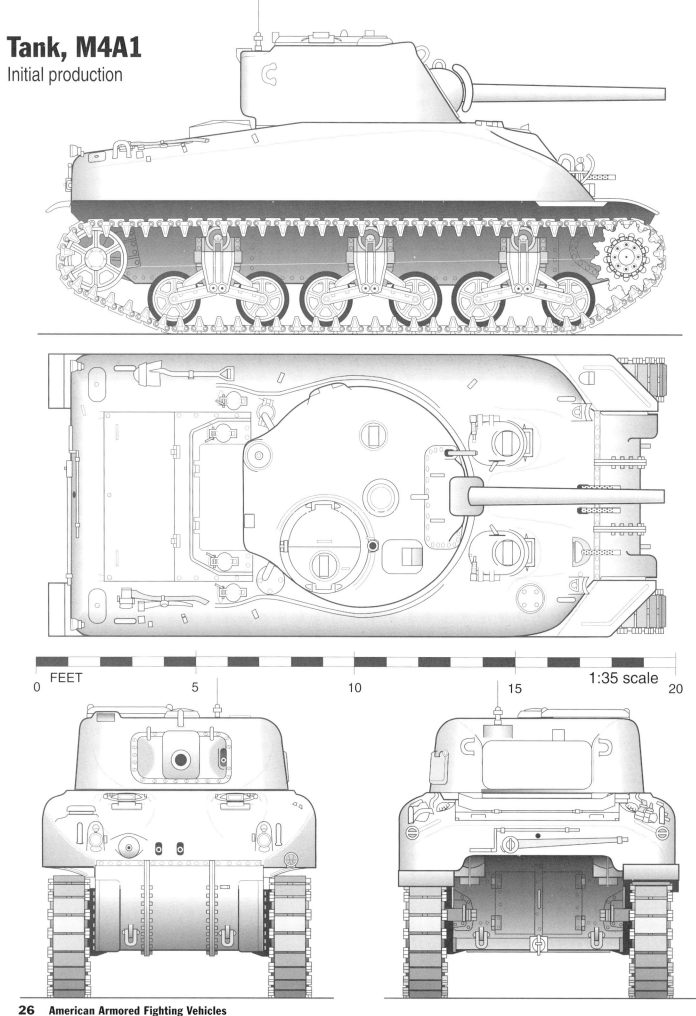

FEET

0   5   10   15   1:35 scale   20

T19 105mm Howitzer Motor Carriage

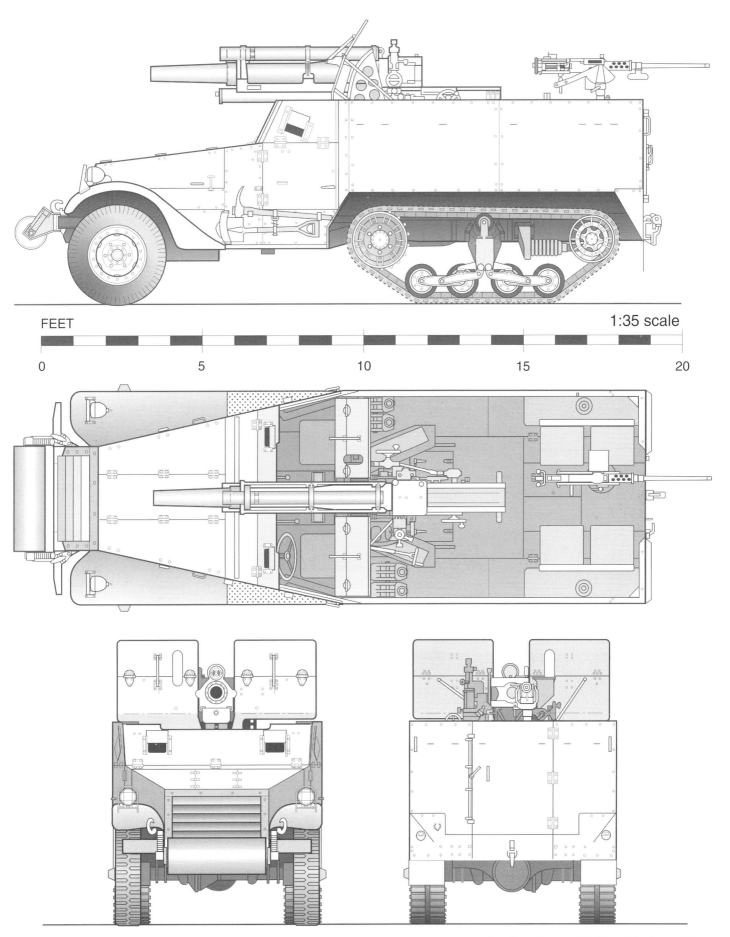

FEET

1:35 scale

0   5   10   15   20

T30 75mm Howitzer Motor Carriage

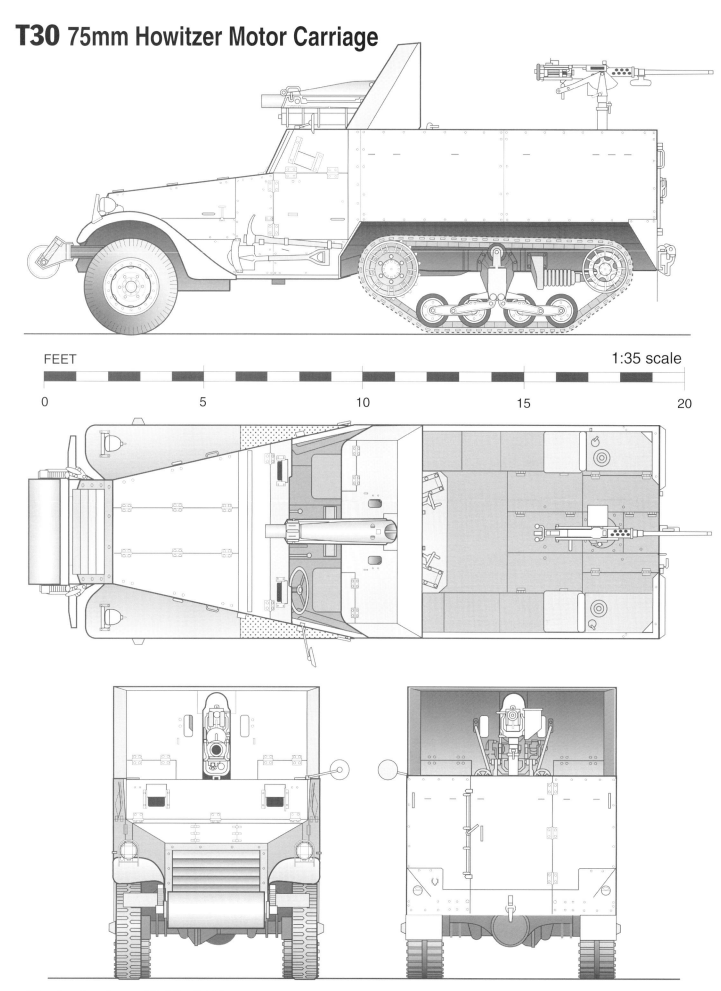

FEET

1:35 scale

0   5   10   15   20

M4 75mm (Dry)

Continental R975 radial engine
Sherman I in British and
Commonwealth service

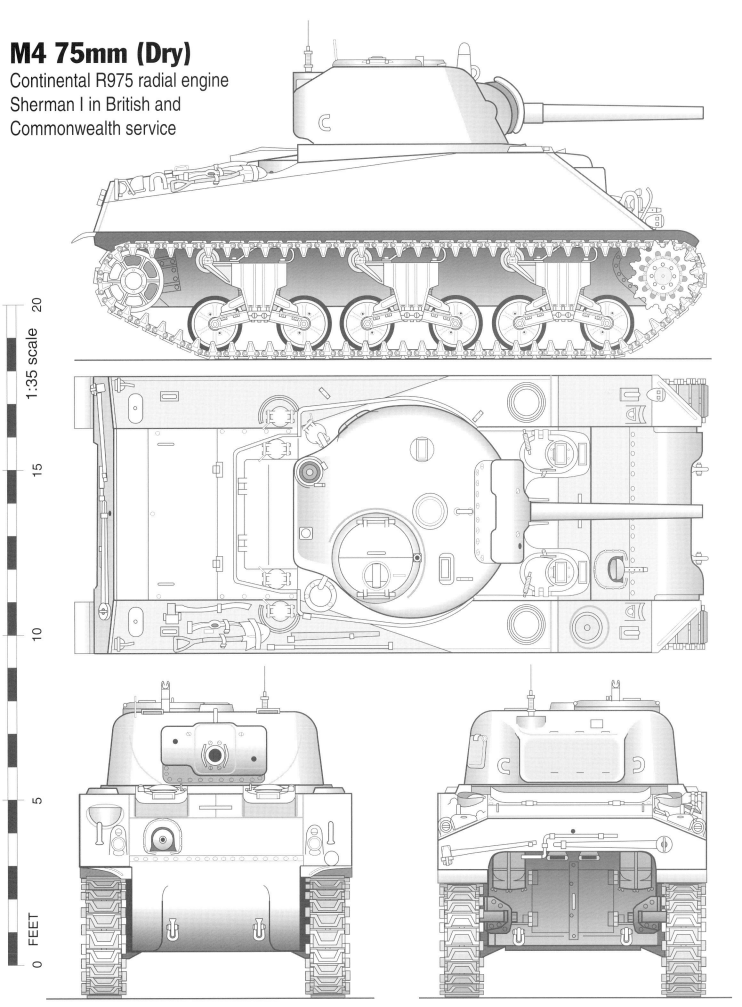

1:35 scale

20

15

10

5

0 FEET

M3 "Lee" Medium Tank

A late production M3 Medium with the long 75mm gun M3 and minus side doors

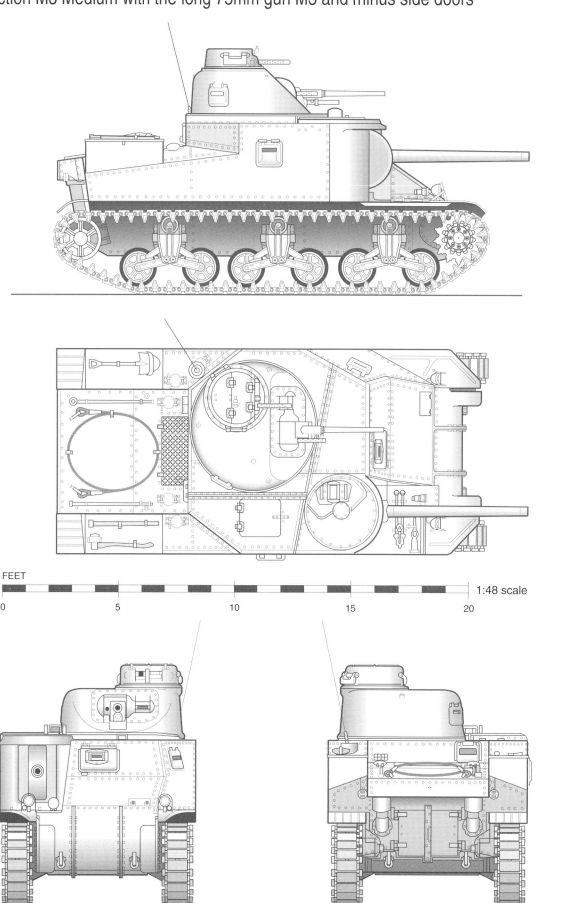

FEET

0   5   10   15   20

1:48 scale

M3A1 "Lee" Medium Tank

A late cast hull M3A1 Medium with ventilators and no side doors

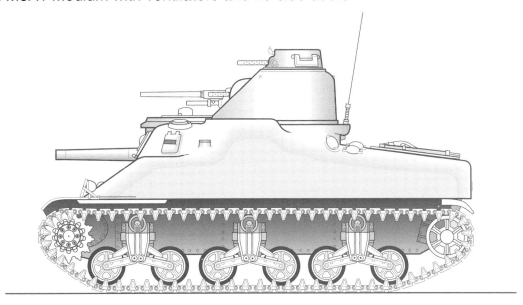

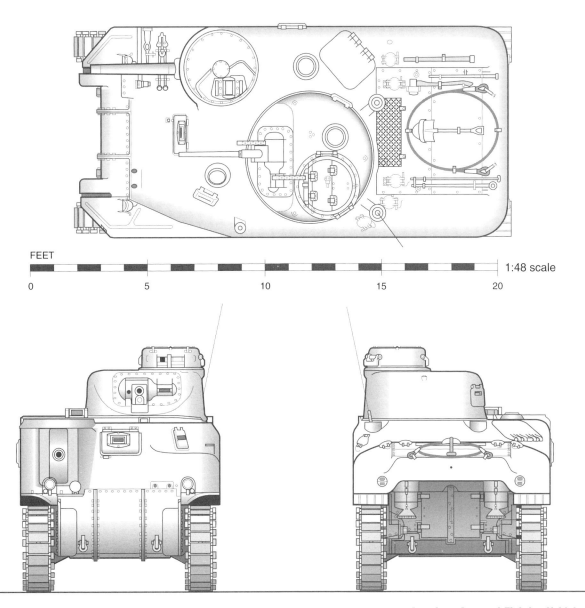

FEET

0   5   10   15   20

1:48 scale

Crew members of an American M3 "Lee" near Souk el Khemis, Tunisia, Nov. 23, 1942. The marking on the front plate designates 1st Armored Division, 13 Armored Regiment, 2nd Battalion, F Company.

Another M3 "Lee" of F Company, 2nd Battalion, 13th Armored Regiment, near Souk el Khemis, Tunisia, Dec. 17, 1942.

Light Tank M3A1

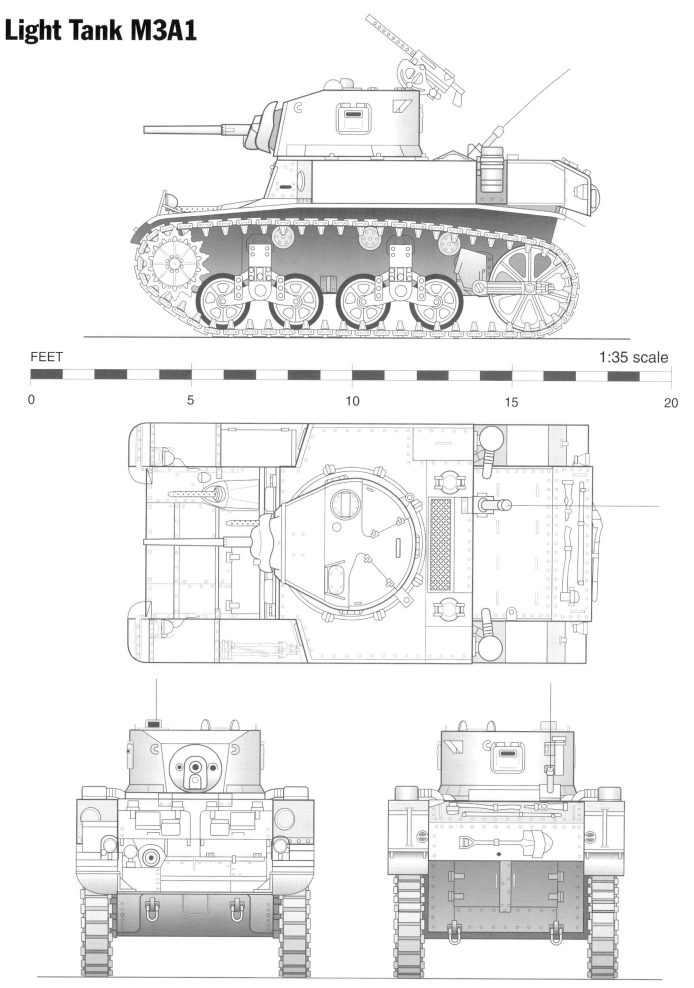

FEET

1:35 scale

0   5   10   15   20

M4A2 75mm (Dry)

mid production GM twin diesel engines
Sherman III in British and
Commonwealth service

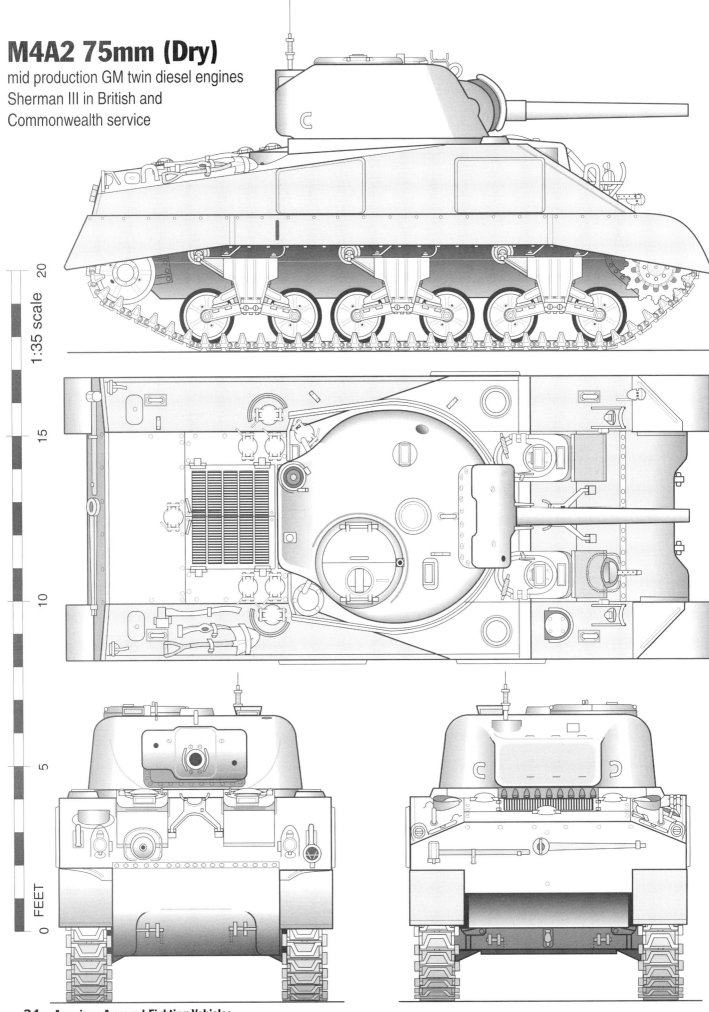

1:35 scale

20

15

10

5

0

FEET

M15 Multiple Gun Motor Carriage

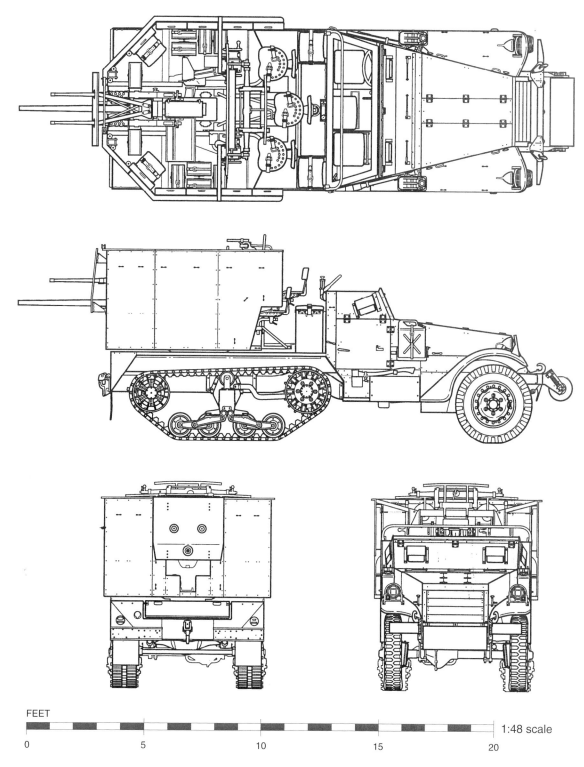

FEET

0   5   10   15   20

1:48 scale

The T28E1 was based on the M3 half-track chassis and would eventually evolve into the M15 Multiple Gun Motor Carriage. It mounted a combination 37mm cannon and .50 cal. machine gun arrangement on a rotating platform. The crew sat in tight quarters when firing the weapons and there was little room for gear other than the top-rounded ammo containers.

The successful employment of the T28E1 in North Africa eventually led to the U.S. Army putting it into full production in early 1943, and 680 were produced under the M15 GMC designation. Giving the crewmen some degree of protection the slab-sided boxy crew compartment made it one of the most easily identified vehicles in the M2/M3 half-track family.

75mm HMC M8 "Scott"

Late Production

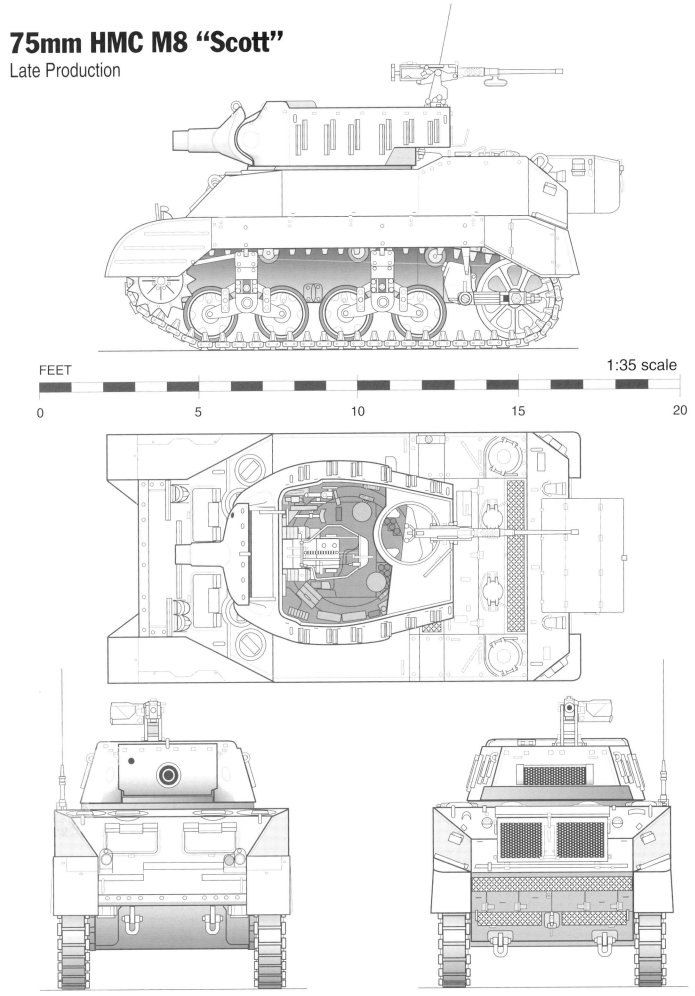

FEET

1:35 scale

0   5   10   15   20

Cargo Carrier M29 Weasel

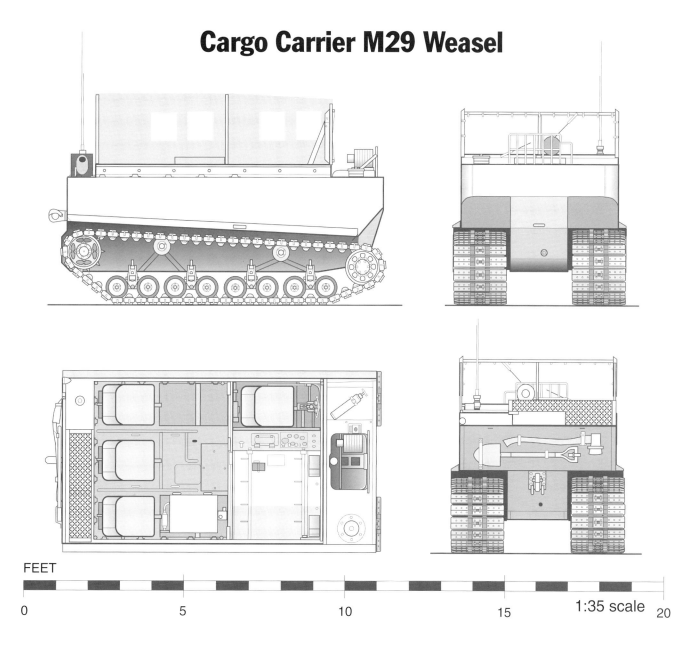

FEET

0   5   10   15   1:35 scale   20

The first practical prototype was designated T15 and it was accepted for production testing. The engine was now mounted in the rear with the 2 center mounted seats still ahead of the engine. The length was shortened approximately 6 feet, the weight was brought down to around 4500 lbs. and the track width was extended to 18 inches. This helped the top speed but the rear mounted engine now made it too heavy in the rear.

The T15 was soon designated M28 and was very similar to its predecessor. Approximately 1,000 T15/M28s were produced between1942 and 1943. Some of these early Weasels were with the 87th Mountain Regiment during the invasion of Kiska Island off the coast of Alaska on August 15, 1942. I should mention here that the Weasel was not armored, its body was spot-welded together with 18-gauge sheet metal.

An almost entirely new Weasel was produced next and the now designated T24 had the engine, once again, mounted amidships with the driver seated to the left of the engine and the gas tank and battery to the right. This left a sizeable area in the rear for seating, cargo and communications equipment. This model had a modified suspension, which now had the bogies set up on 4 transverse mounted leaf springs. The drive

sprocket was moved to the rear, and another new body design made the vehicle appear like it was going backwards. This body was also made of 18-gauge steel.

With the new body, suspension, engine, and seating arrangement, the Weasels fast paced development finally paid off. It did however still have a tendency to throw a track now and then. The T24 soon evolved into the M29, but overall they were very much the same. The M29 would float but it was quite slow and did not steer well in the water.

The Weasel proved to be very popular with the troops. One of its many uses was as an ambulance. The Weasel could be fitted with up to four stretchers. The GI's knew that unique clattering "Weasel sound" and as supplies were brought up to the front the wounded were taken back. The Weasel soldiered on for many years, from the Aleutian and Pacific Islands all the way through Italy, France, Belgium and Germany. After WWII the Weasel rolled on through Korea as well. A number of vehicles ended up in Norway and were used there until 1984. The French also used Weasels during the Southeast Asia conflict. Here they were called "Crabs".

M2A1 Half-track Car

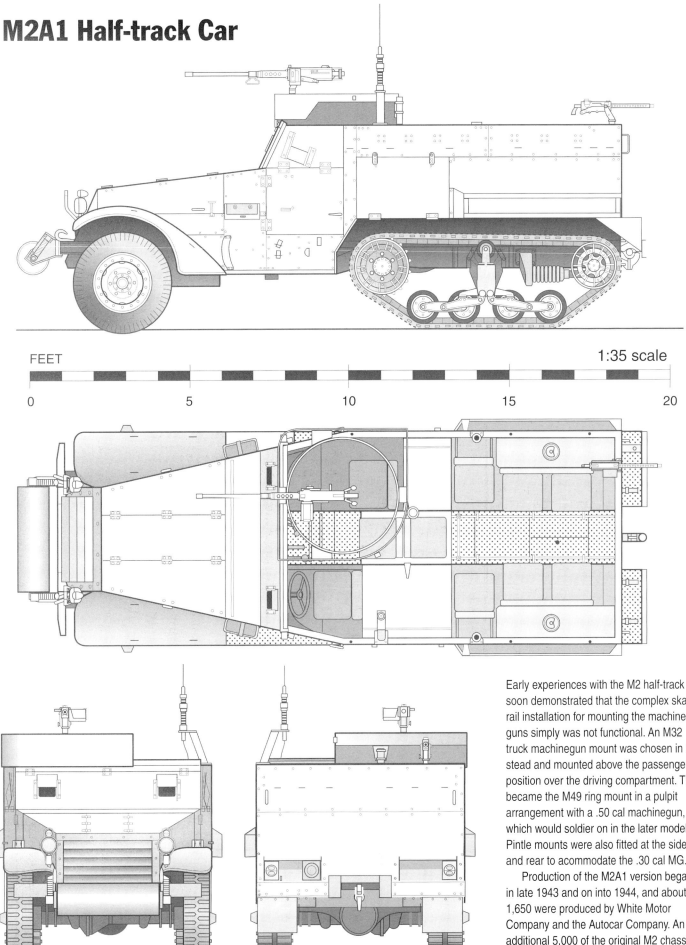

FEET

1:35 scale

0   5   10   15   20

Early experiences with the M2 half-track soon demonstrated that the complex skate rail installation for mounting the machineguns simply was not functional. An M32 truck machinegun mount was chosen in its stead and mounted above the passenger's position over the driving compartment. This became the M49 ring mount in a pulpit arrangement with a .50 cal machinegun, which would soldier on in the later models. Pintle mounts were also fitted at the sides and rear to acommodate the .30 cal MG.

Production of the M2A1 version began in late 1943 and on into 1944, and about 1,650 were produced by White Motor Company and the Autocar Company. An additional 5,000 of the original M2 chassis were also refitted as M2A1s.

M9A1 Half-Track
Built by International Harvester Company

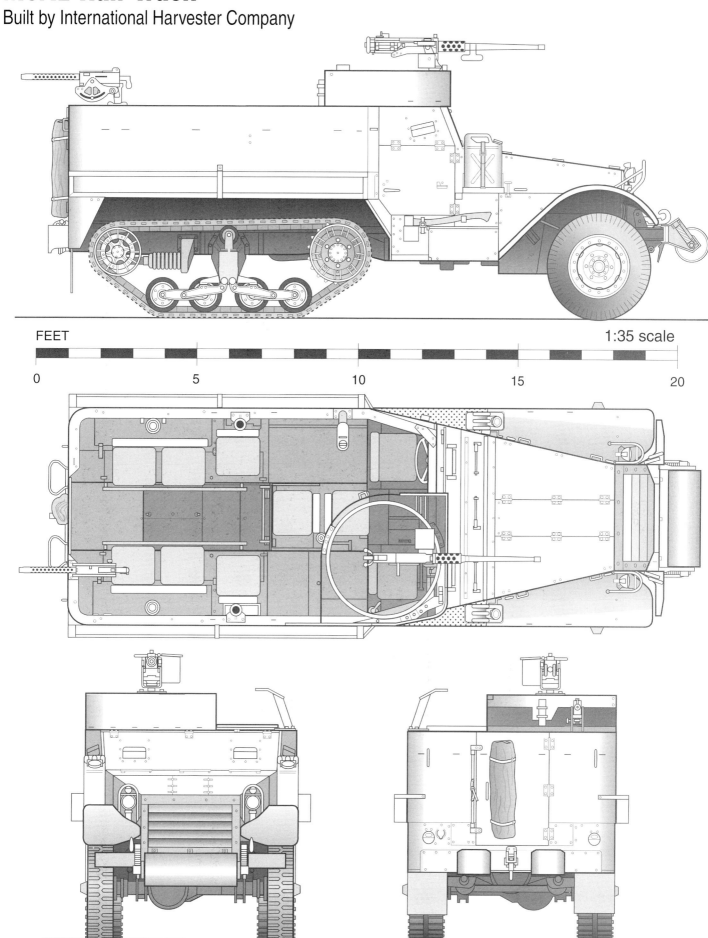

FEET

1:35 scale

0   5   10   15   20

M9A1 Half-Track
Mainly in British and Commonwealth Service

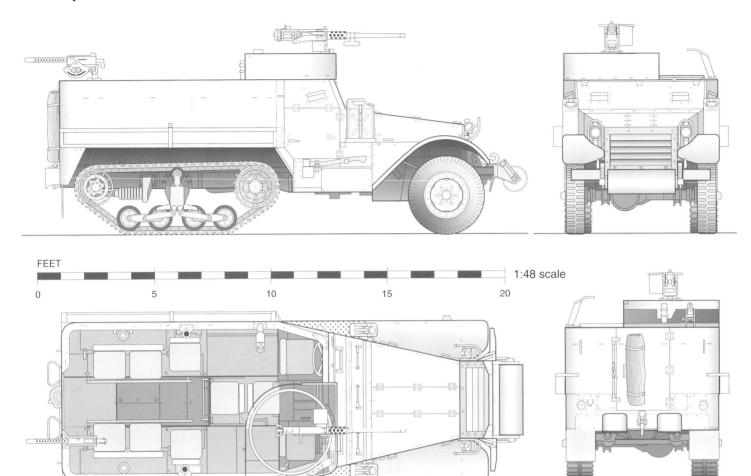

FEET

1:48 scale

0   5   10   15   20

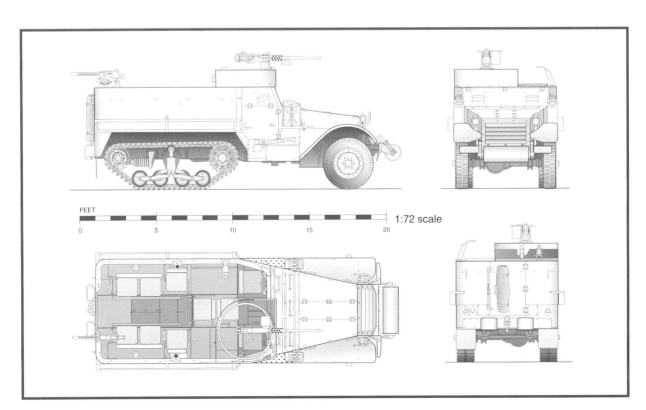

FEET

1:72 scale

0   5   10   15   20

M3A4 "Lee", Medium Tank

A late production M3A4 with extended chassis, ventilators, heavy duty suspension, and Chrysler A57 multibank engine

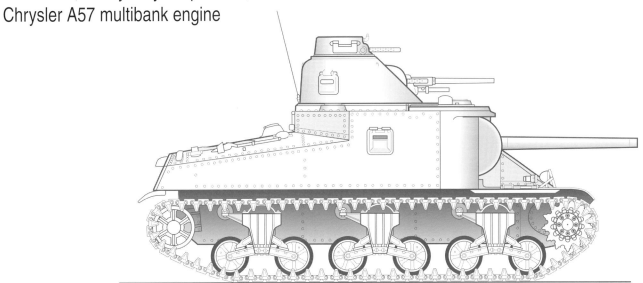

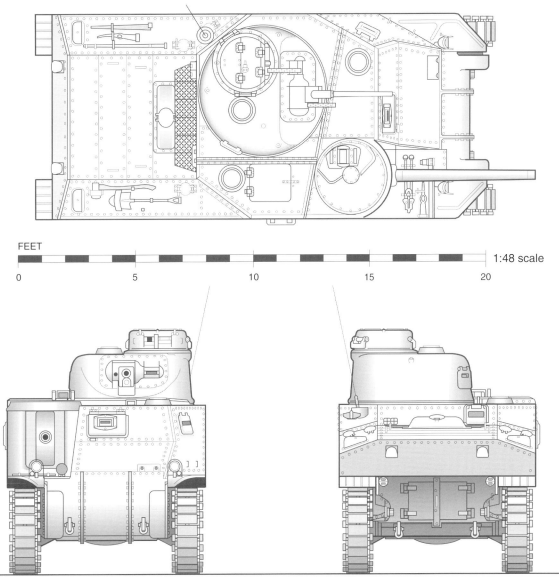

FEET

0   5   10   15   20

1:48 scale

Armored Car, T13

(Son of Trackless Tank)

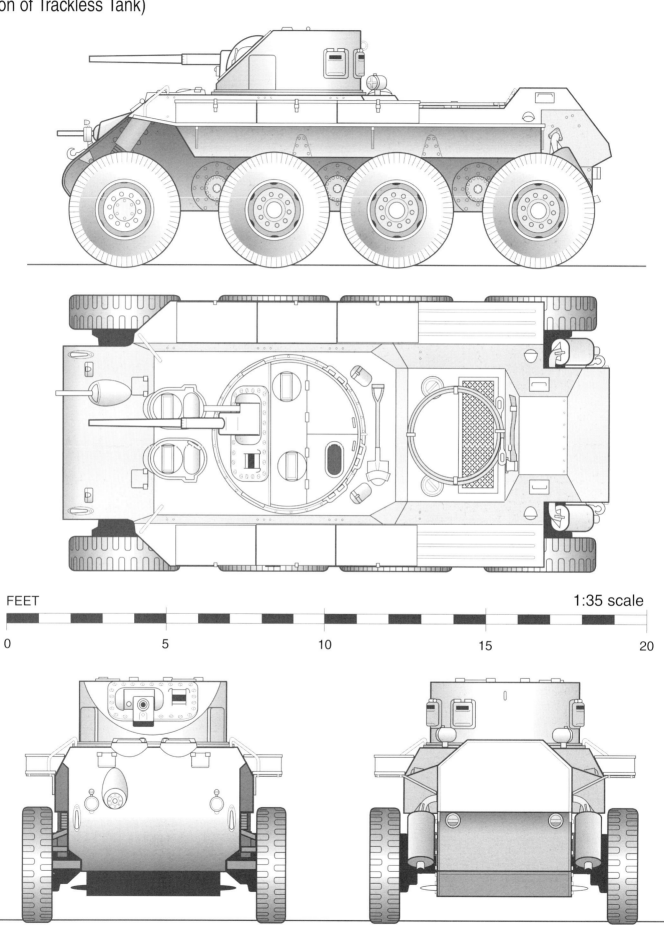

FEET

1:35 scale

0   5   10   15   20

T17 Deerhound
Medium Armored Car

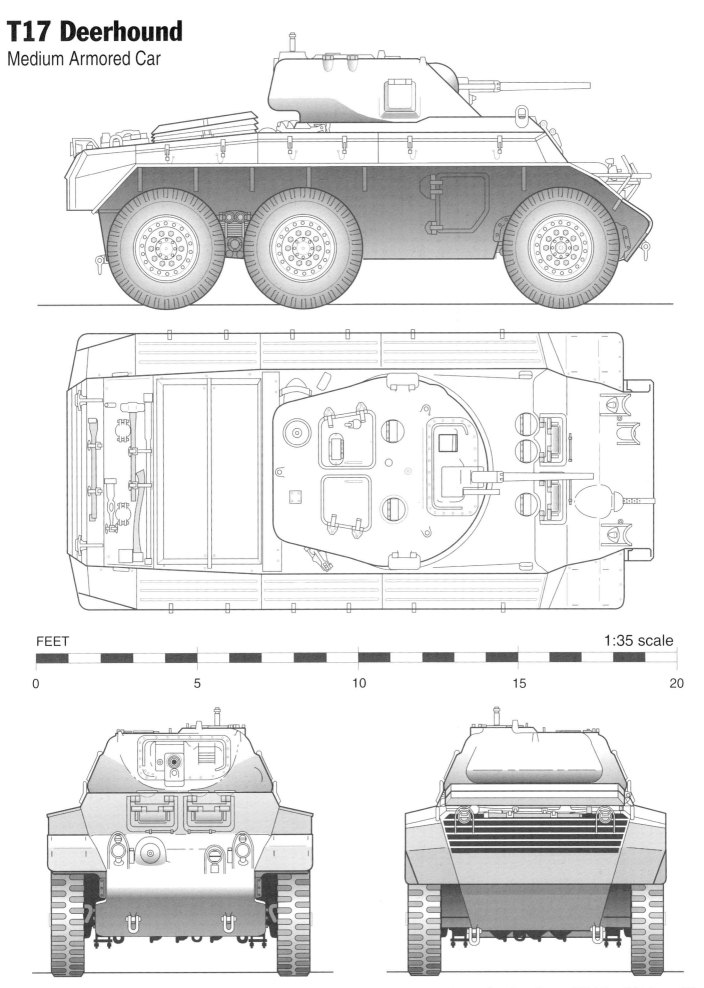

FEET

1:35 scale

0   5   10   15   20

T24 Scout Car

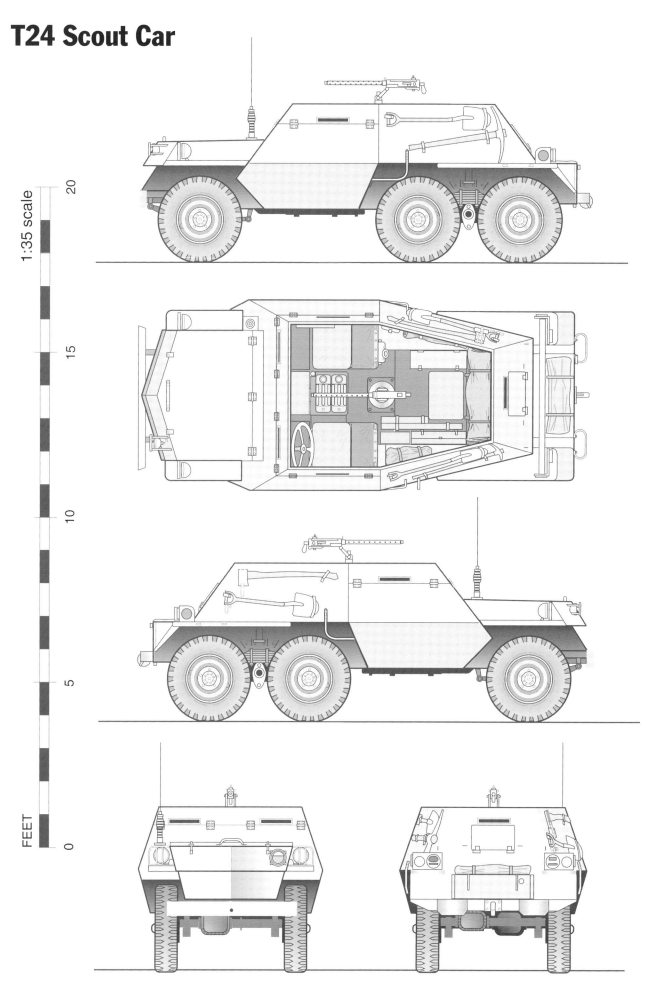

1:35 scale

FEET

20

15

10

5

0

Armoured Car, Staghound I (T17E1)
In Canadian and British Service

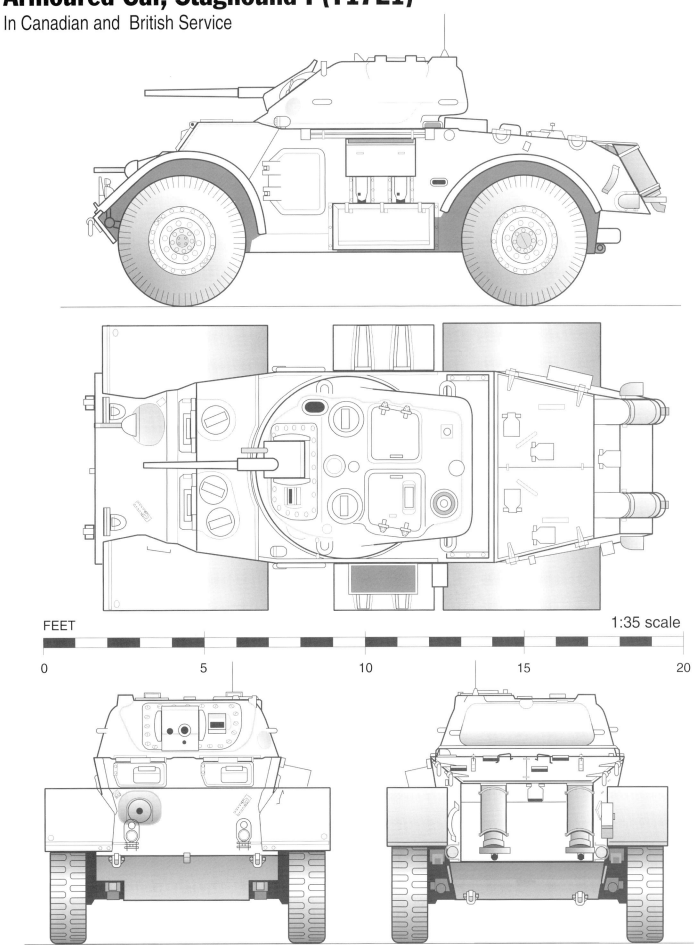

FEET

1:35 scale

0   5   10   15   20

A group of Canadian Staghound armored cars of the 12th Manitoba Dragoons negotiating
an abandoned railway line in the area of the Hochwald Forest, Germany, March 7, 1945.

Armoured Car, AA, Staghound (T17E2)
In Canadian and British Service
(Fraser-Nash turret, armed with Browning .5 cal. MGs)

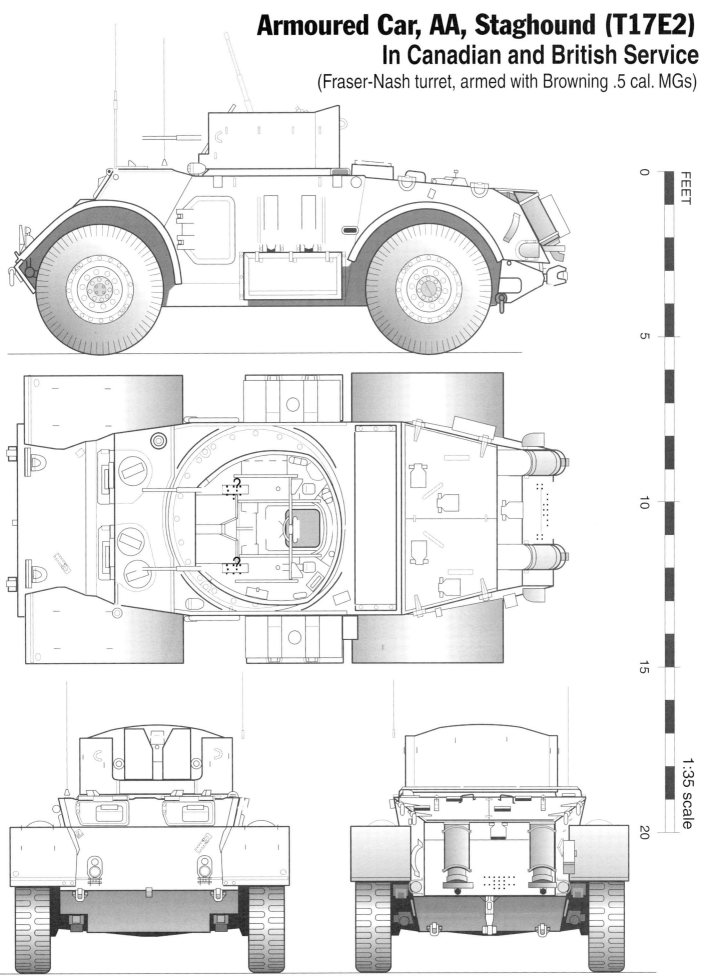

FEET

0

5

10

15

20

1:35 scale

Grant I Cruiser Tank
The American M3 medium tank built for British service, North Africa 1942

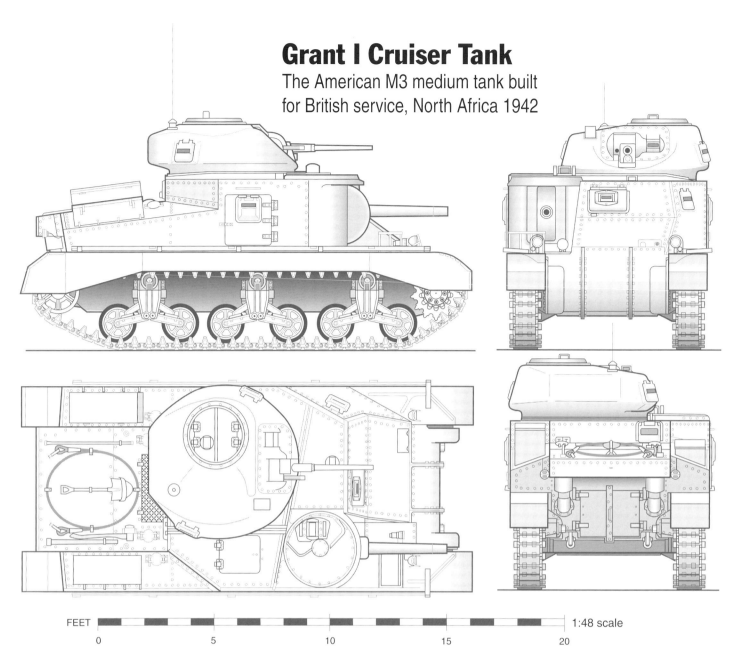

FEET   0   5   10   15   20   1:48 scale

The Grant tank was basically the U.S. M3 medium tank built to British specifications. A rather more sleek, wider and lower cast turret was developed, and the commander's cupola was done away with. The overhang in the rear of the turret was built to accommodate a radio.

They first made their appearance with 1st and 7th Armoured Divisions where over 150 of them fought during the Gazala battles of May-June 1942. This was the first tank the Eighth Army had with a powerful 75 mm gun firing both armor-piercing and high explosive rounds, and could also outrange the majority of German Pz. III and IV models. This advantage would not last too long, but they definitely made themselves felt when taking out German anti-tank guns. The Grant would soon be replaced by the Sherman, but many of them soldiered on in the Burma theater, and with Australian troops in the southwest Pacific well after they had disappeared from the western front battles.

U.S. service crew unload shells from General Grant tanks at the Heliopolis repair depot, Egypt, December 1942. These tanks are in for a complete overhaul in December 1942 following the El Alamein battles and pursuit.(SC)

M31(T2) ARV
On early M3 medium with dummy guns

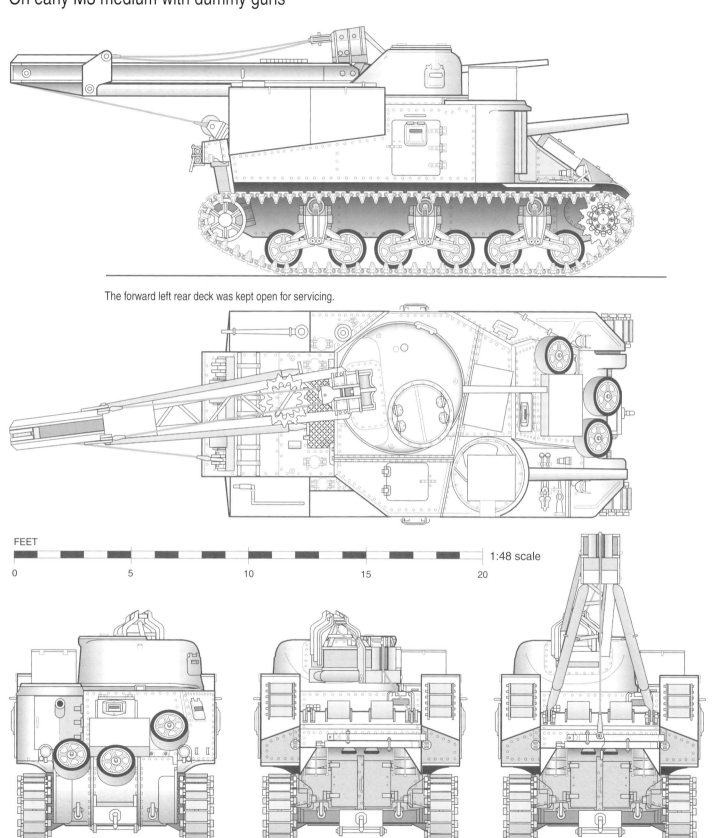

The forward left rear deck was kept open for servicing.

FEET

0   5   10   15   20

1:48 scale

The front sponson door opens to the right.

The boom jack legs could also be extended to rest on the ground with the aid of foot assemblies, to handle even heavier loads.

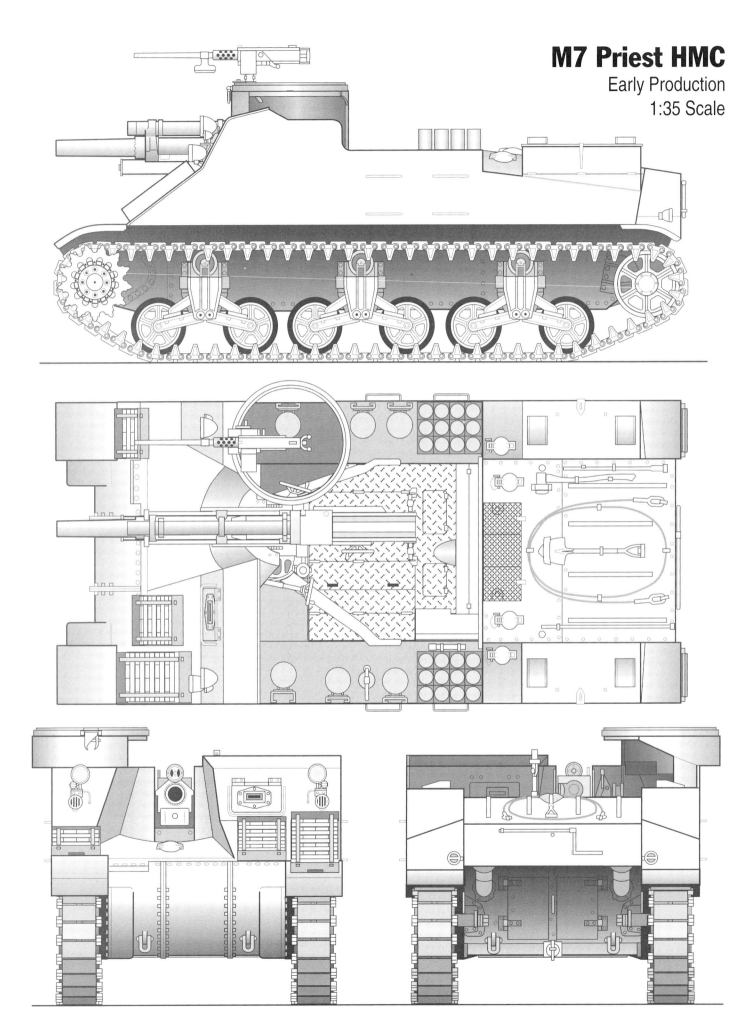

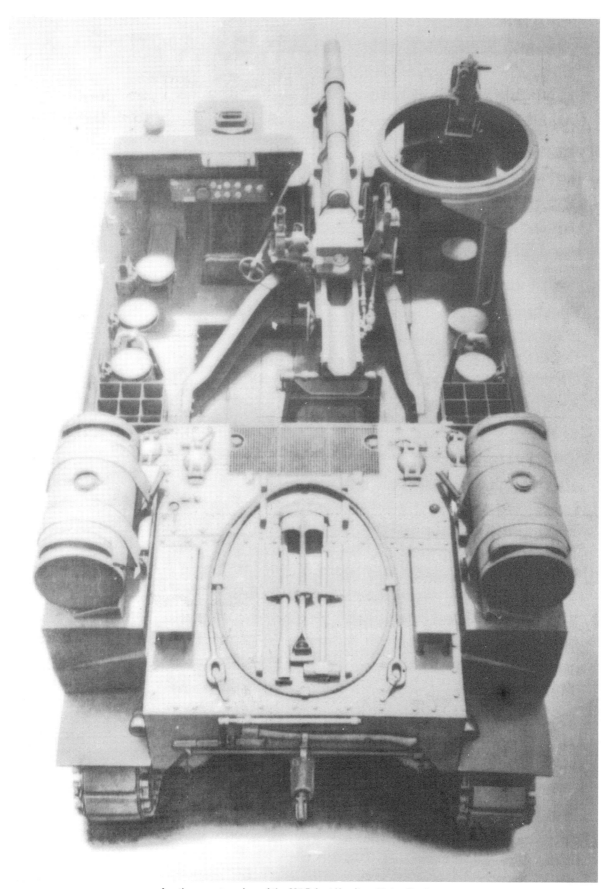

A rather rare top view of the M7 Priest Howitzer Motor Carriage.

Cargo Carrier M29C "Weasel"

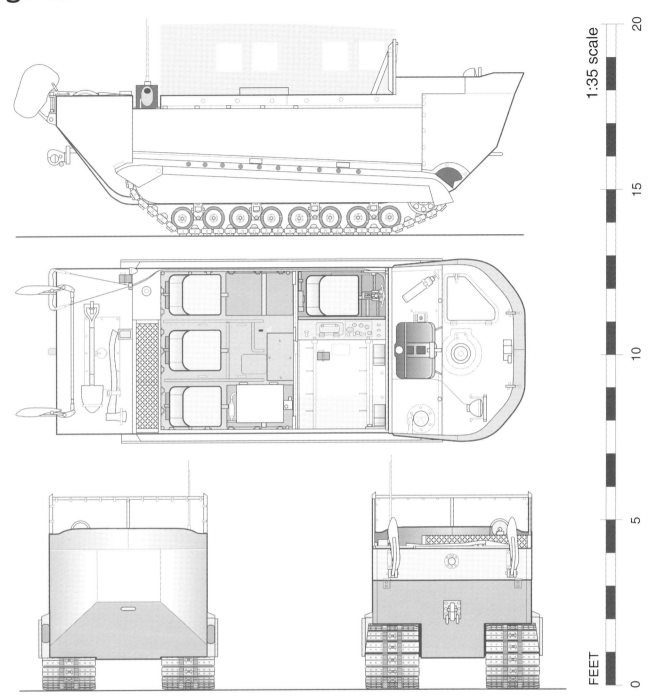

1:35 scale

FEET

With the new body, suspension, engine, and seating arrangement of the M29, the Weasel's fast paced development finally paid off. It did however still have a tendency to throw a track now and then. The M29 would float but it was quite slow and did not steer well in the water. A new model of Weasel soon evolved designated the M29C.

New front and rear flotation tanks were added to help the Weasel travel through water with more freeboard and speed. The bow tank was shaped like a boat's hull and carried a surf guard to keep water from entering the vehicle in rough water. If there was ever a time that the Weasel could not climb a slippery bank or make it up a steep slope, a PTO driven capstan winch was mounted on top of the bow flotation tank. The stern tank carried twin rudders controlled by a tiller at the front of the driver's station for improved steering. These rudders could be raised and secured for travel on land.

Problems with water turbulence created by the tracks running backward on the upper track run was helped but not entirely eliminated by adding side skirts,

which channeled the water out and to the sides of the vehicle. The M29C was the last variant produced and there were a total of 15,124 units built between 1942 and 1945. There were always experimental vehicles being tested with a variety of weapons and devices such as machine guns, recoilless rifles and mine clearing devices.

The Weasel proved to be very popular with the troops. One of its many uses was as an ambulance. The Weasel could be fitted with up to four stretchers. The GI's knew that unique clattering "Weasel sound" and as supplies were brought up to the front the wounded were taken back. The Weasel soldiered on for many years, from the Aleutian and Pacific Islands all the way through Italy, France, Belgium and Germany. After WWII the Weasel rolled on through Korea as well. A number of vehicles ended up in Norway and were used there until 1984. The French also used Weasels during the Southeast Asia conflict. Here they were called "Crabs".

M8 Light Armored Car

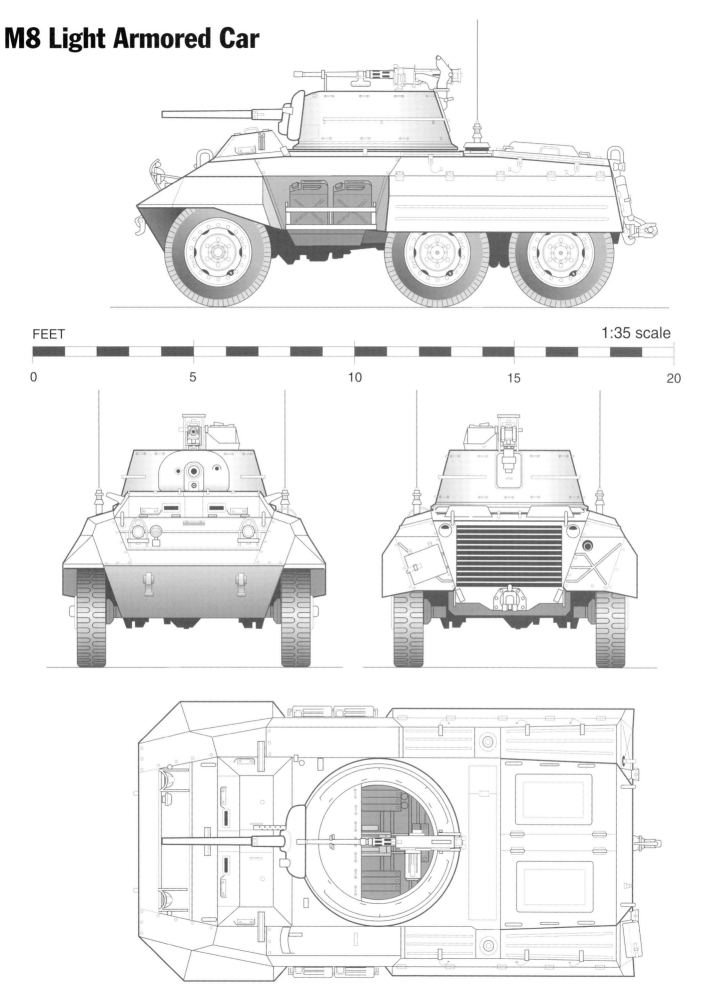

FEET

1:35 scale

0   5   10   15   20

Two excellent views of an M8 Light Armored Car on display at Fort Hood, Texas.

M6A1 (Welded Hull)
Heavy Tank

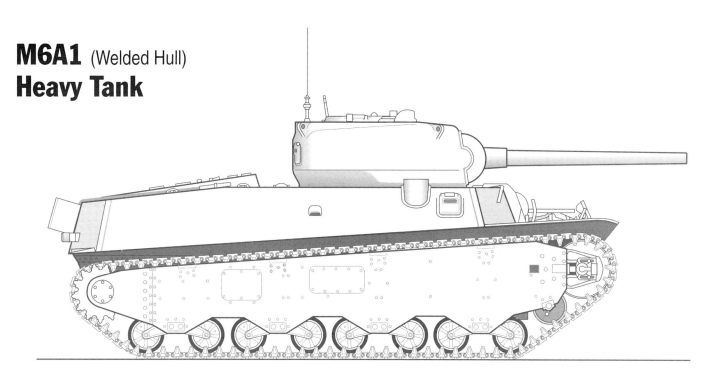

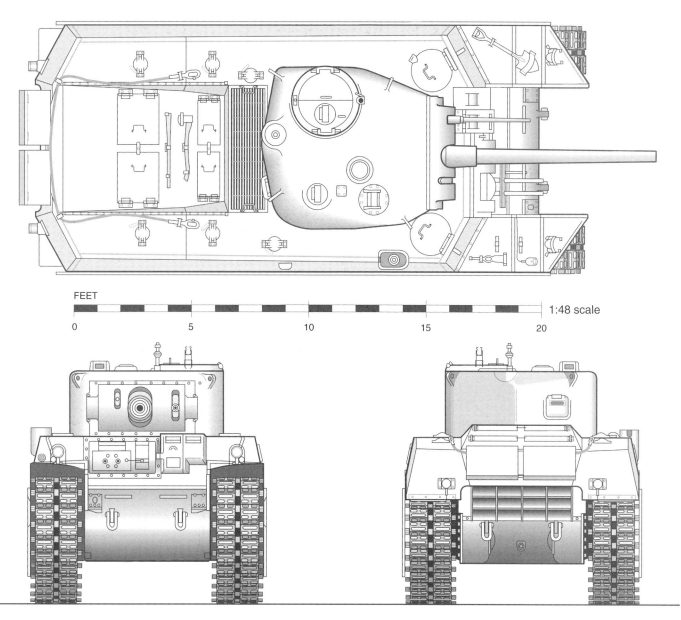

FEET

0   5   10   15   20

1:48 scale

M15A1 Combination Gun Motor Carriage

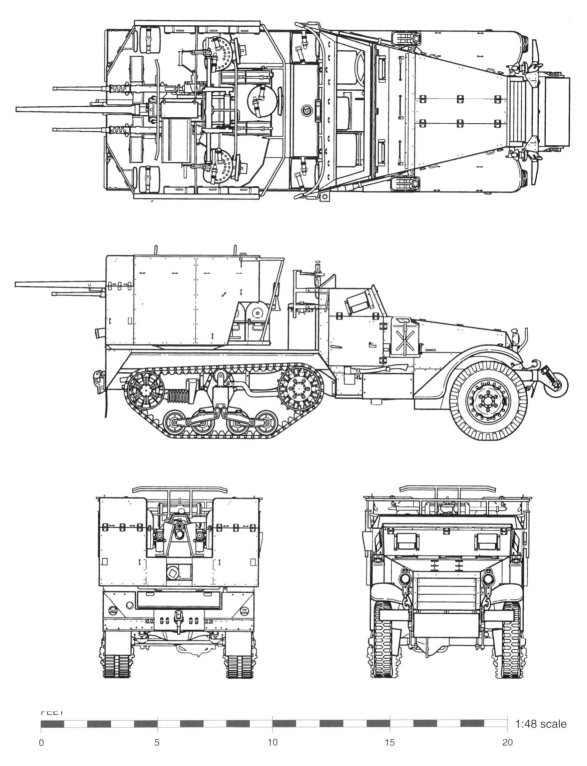

FEET

0   5   10   15   20

1:48 scale

The M15A1 was simply an upgraded M15 featuring an improved fire control system and changes to the M3 chassis to handle the increased weight. The .50 calibre machine guns were repositioned under the 37mm cannon, and forward visibility was improved by employing a fold-down armored shield at the top of the front sides. The front of the fighting compartment often faced to the rear when in transit.

At this point the designation was now changed to combination gun motor carriage M15E1 with combination gun mount T87. A grip rail was added to the rear of the mount to aid the crew when mounting and dismounting. The production M15A1 was by far the most common of the three variants built and more that 1,600 came off the assembly lines between late 1943 and early 1944.

M20 Armored Command Car
(Armored Utility Car, M10)

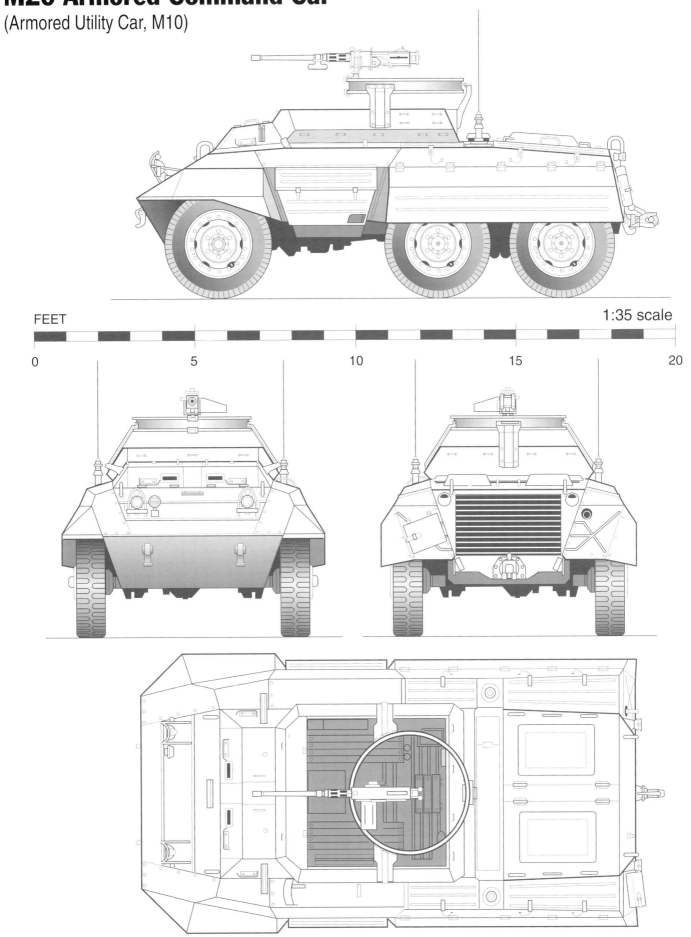

FEET

1:35 scale

0   5   10   15   20

M4A3 75mm Wet

Ford GAA engine
Sherman IV if in British
and Commonwealth service

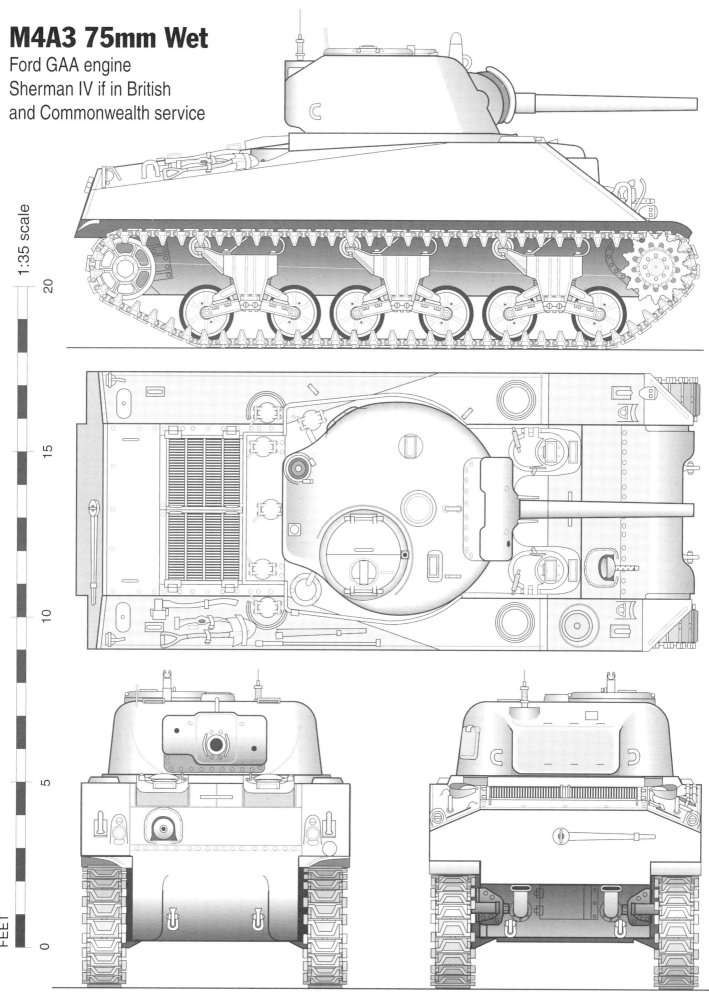

1:35 scale

FEET

Light Tank M3A3 "Stuart V"

The M3A3 Stuart was being developed in parallel, and along similar lines as the M5 light tank. The M5 had evolved from the M3E3, and to avoid confusion with the newly arriving M4 medium tank, it was designated as light tank M5 rather than repeating M4.

The M5 was chosen for the U.S. Army, and the M3A3 was directed to foreign aid. Both Britain and Canada accepted the M3A3 as their standard light tank and received over 2100 of these vehicles. Another 1000 were allocated to Nationalist China, and 277 went to the Free French forces which were now a sizeable Allied force. Once production permitted, the M5A1 Stuart VI was also issued to British units.

In British and Canadian service the M3A3 light tank was designated as Stuart V, and saw service in both the Western European theatre and Italy. It was normally used by Armoured Regiments and Armoured Reconnaissance Regiments to feel out enemy positions on a regimental front.

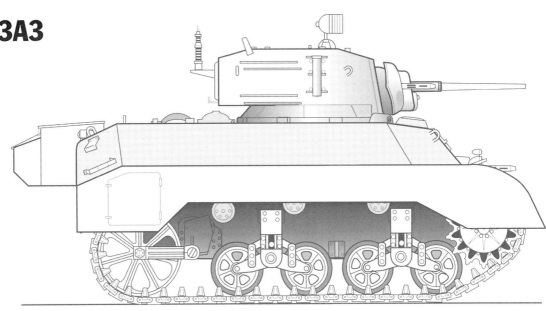

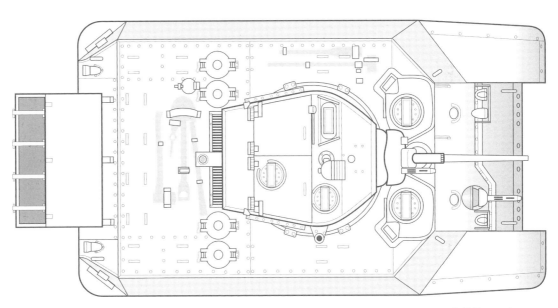

FEET

0   5   10   15   20

1:35 scale

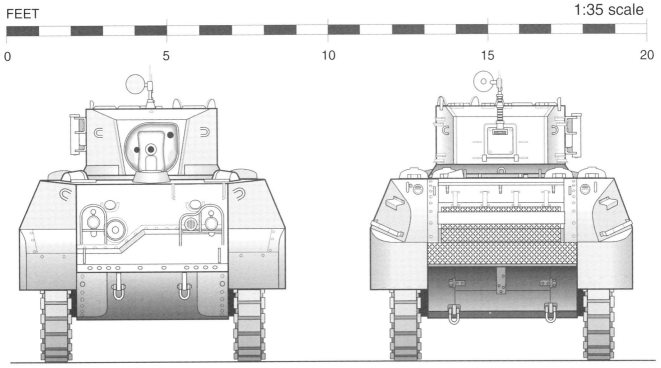

M4A4 75mm (Dry)

remanufactured Chrysler A57
multibank engine Sherman V
in British and Commonwealth service

1:35 scale

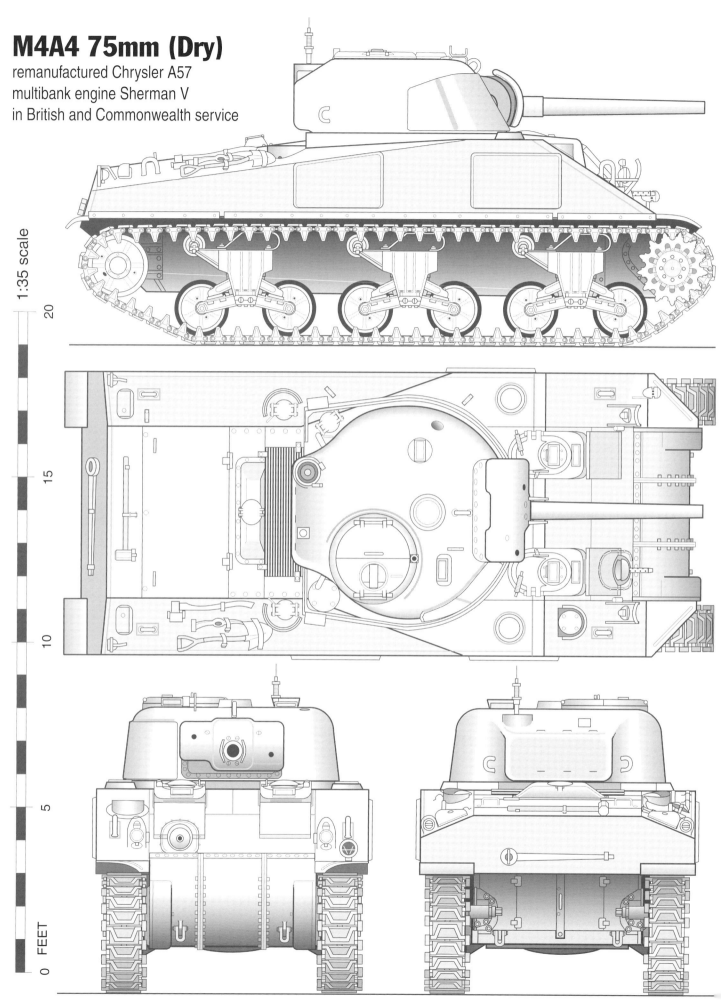

M12 155mm Gun Motor Carriage

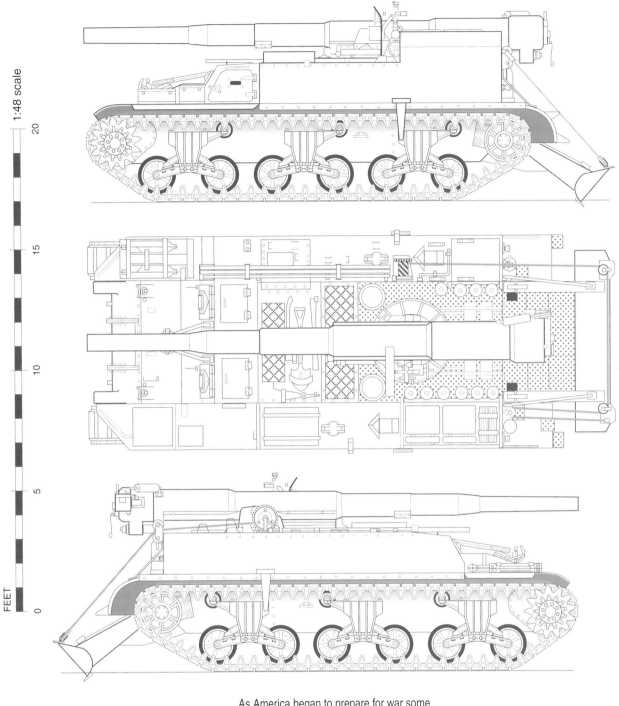

1:48 scale

FEET

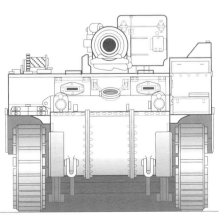

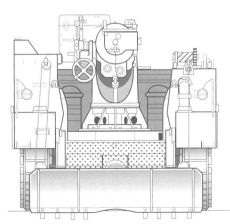

As America began to prepare for war some planners quickly realized that there would be a need for self-propelled heavy artillery that could keep up with the tanks. The French designed 155 mm gun M.1918 from WWI service was chosen to be fitted to a modified M3 Medium Tank chassis bed. By early 1943 the M12 was in production but still was not fully appreciated by the Army Ground Forces, who had had no real experience with the use of self propelled artillery. Eventually they were won over and the M12 proved to be one of the more important weapons on the western front.

M30 Cargo Carrier

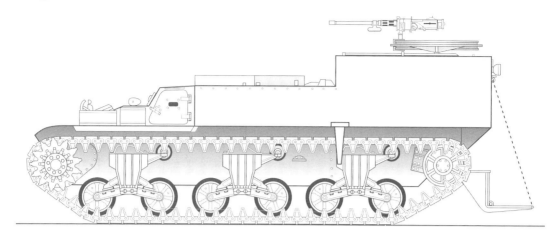

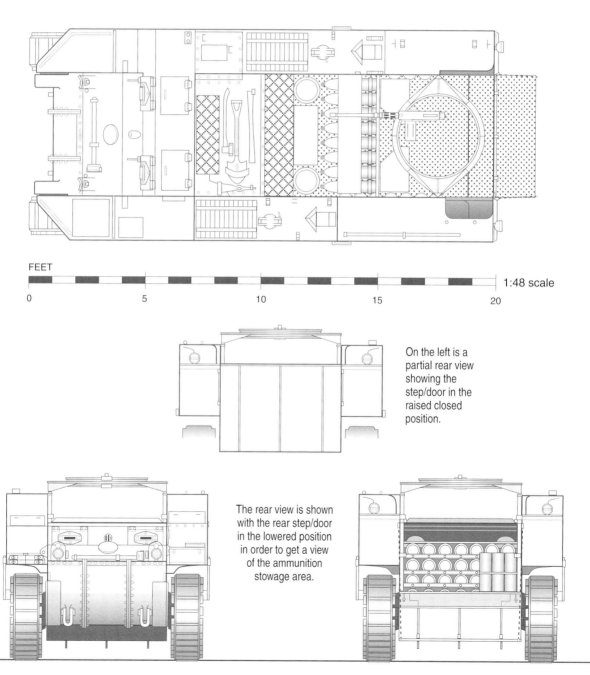

FEET

1:48 scale

0   5   10   15   20

On the left is a partial rear view showing the step/door in the raised closed position.

The rear view is shown with the rear step/door in the lowered position in order to get a view of the ammunition stowage area.

Light Tank M5A1
early production with Culin hedgerow cutter

The M5 evolved from the M3E3, and to avoid confusion with the newly arriving M4 medium tanks, it was wisely designated as light tank M5 rather than repeating M4. Production of the M5 began in April 1942 and roughly 2074 were produced by December 1942. The new improved turret developed for the M3A3 provided room for an SCR 508 radio in the rear bustle, and a similar approach was taken for the M5A1 turret. By June 1944 a total of 6810 of the M5A1 model had been built.

The M5A1 was chosen for the U.S. Army, and the M3A3 was directed to foreign aid. However, once production permitted, the M5A1 Stuart VI was also issued to British units.

This M5A1 is fitted with the Culin hedgerow cutter, a device welded together from German angle iron beach obstacles. Its purpose was to cut through the root masses found in Normandy's hedgerow district. They were named after Sgt. Curtis Culin who created this ingenious device.

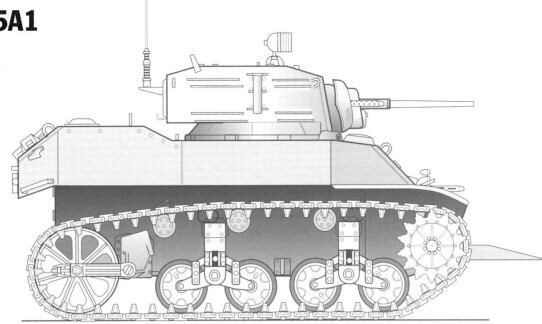

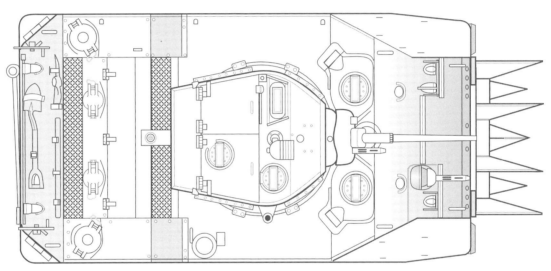

FEET

1:35 scale

0   5   10   15   20

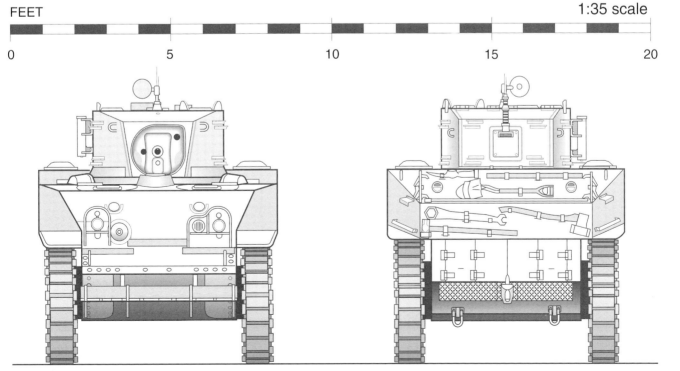

M10 3 inch Gun Motor Carriage
mid-production

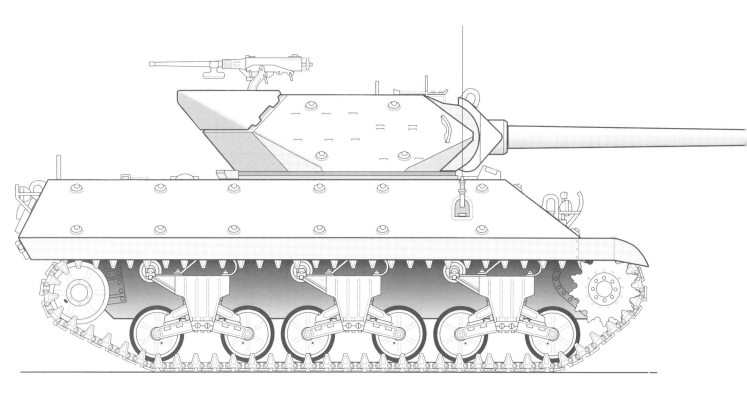

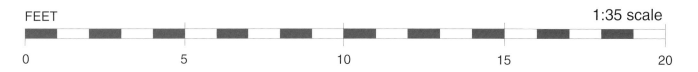

FEET   1:35 scale

0   5   10   15   20

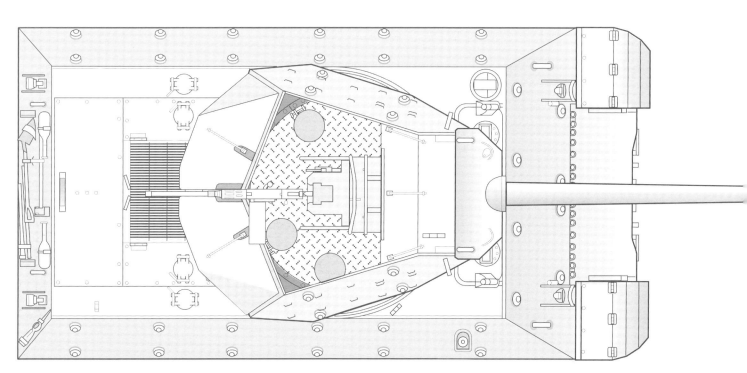

M10 3 inch Gun Motor Carriage

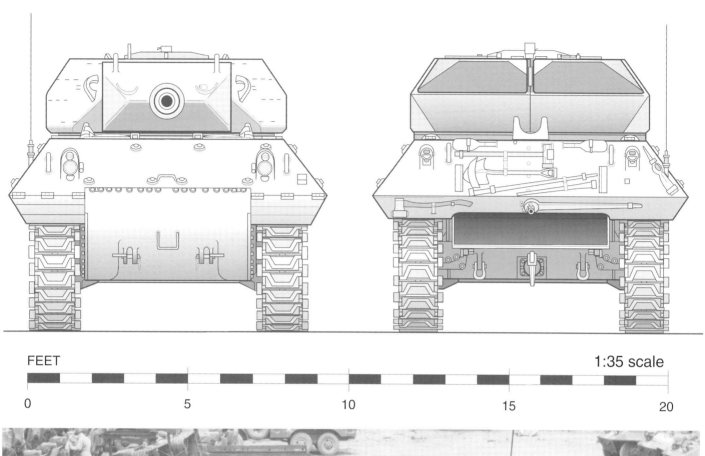

FEET   1:35 scale

0   5   10   15   20

An interesting view of an American M10 Gun Motor Carriage with the 3 inch L/53 gun, and crewmen in full regalia.
The vehicle name in white letter just ahead of the aerial mount reads "BOUNCING TNT".

M4A1(76) Wet Sherman

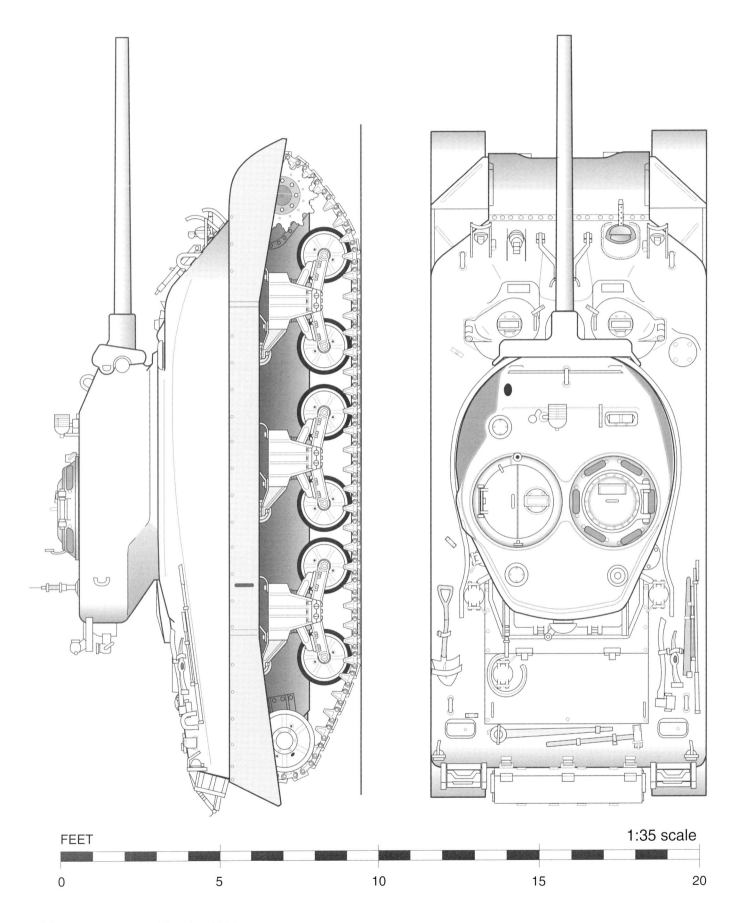

FEET

1:35 scale

0   5   10   15   20

M4A1(76) Wet Sherman

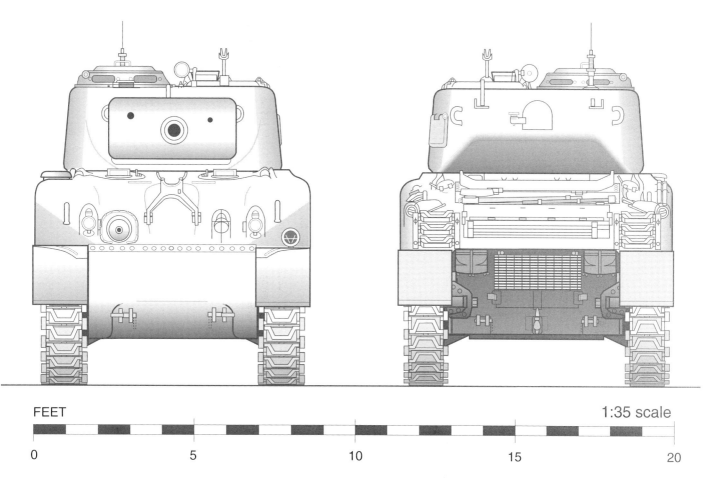

FEET   1:35 scale

0   5   10   15   20

Assault Tank M4A3E2 "Jumbo"

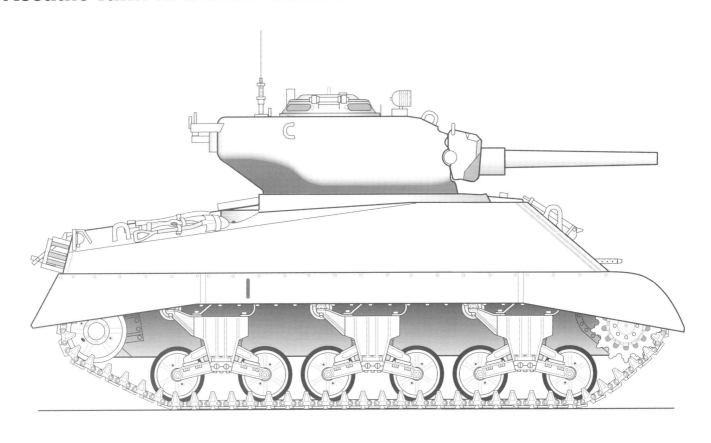

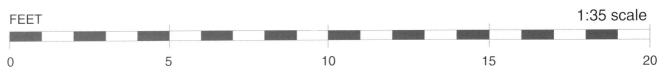

FEET

1:35 scale

0   5   10   15   20

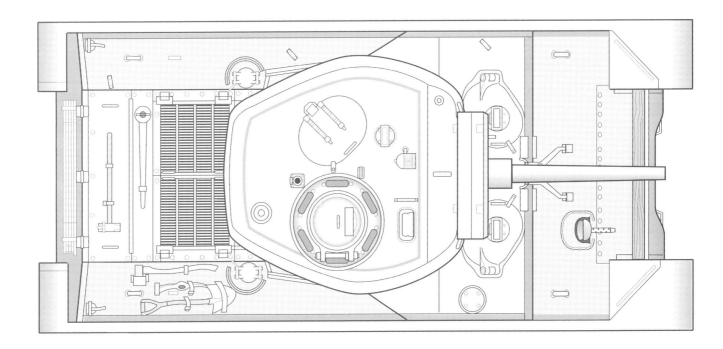

Assault Tank M4A3E2

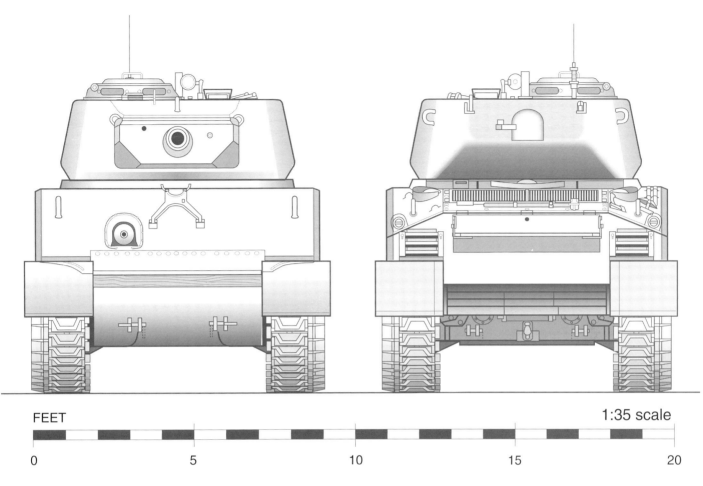

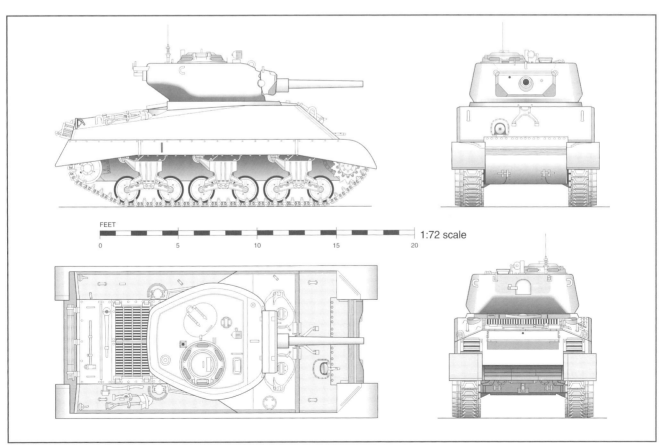

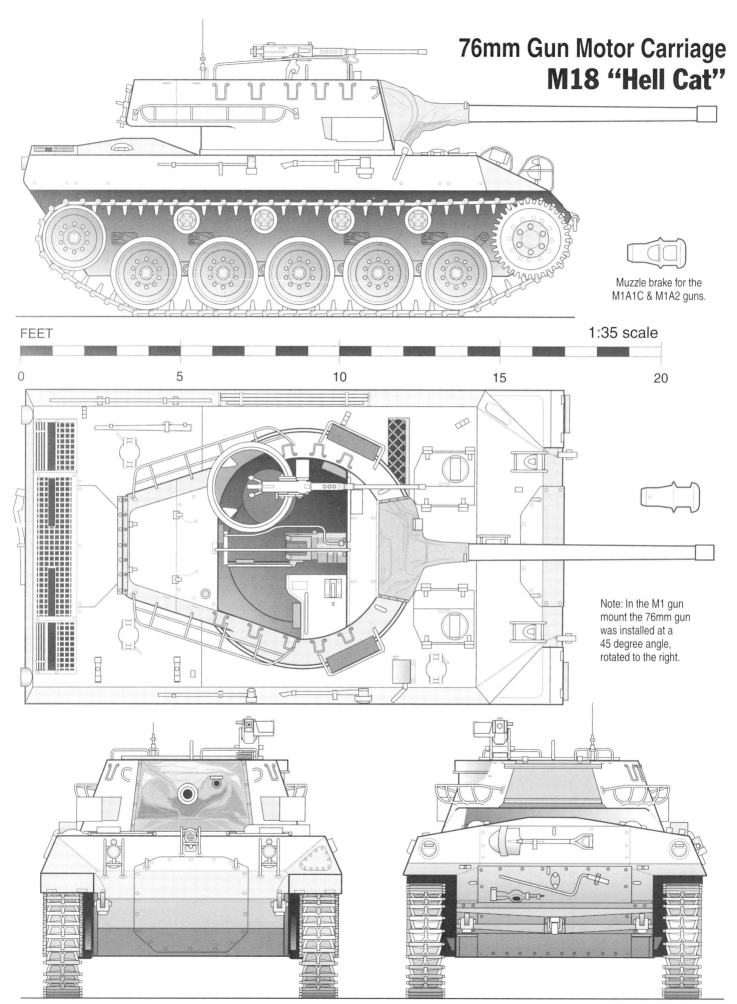

76mm Gun Motor Carriage
M18 "Hell Cat"

Muzzle brake for the
M1A1C & M1A2 guns.

FEET

1:35 scale

0   5   10   15   20

Note: In the M1 gun
mount the 76mm gun
was installed at a
45 degree angle,
rotated to the right.

M3A2 Half-Track

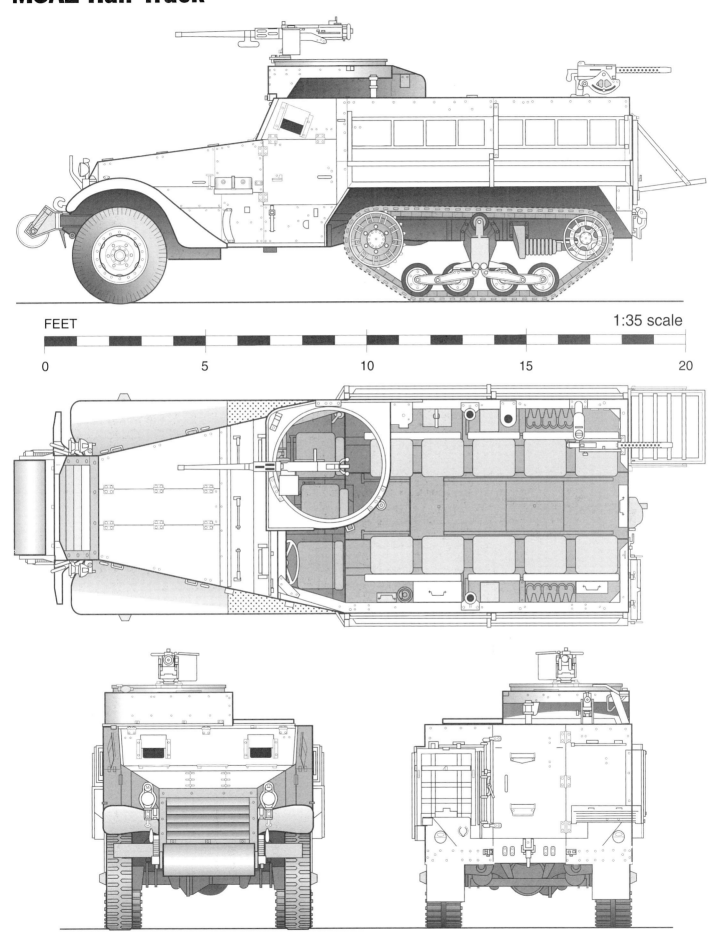

FEET

1:35 scale

0   5   10   15   20

M4A2(76) Wet Sherman

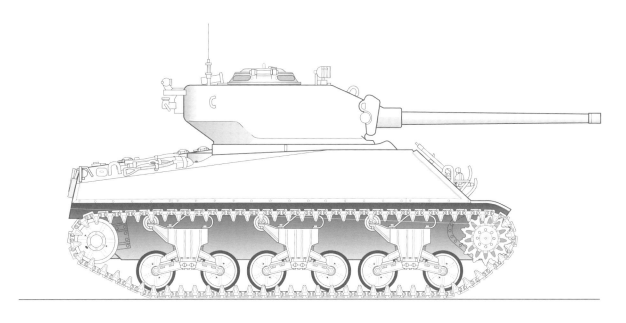

FEET

1:48 scale

0   5   10   15   20

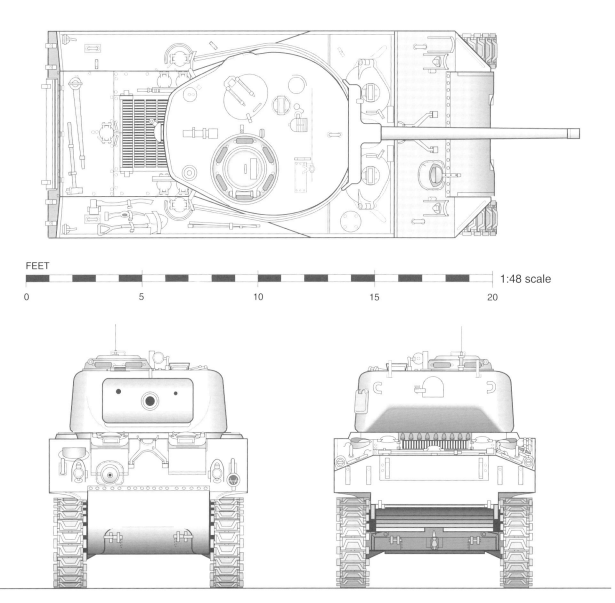

Armored Utility Vehicle
M39

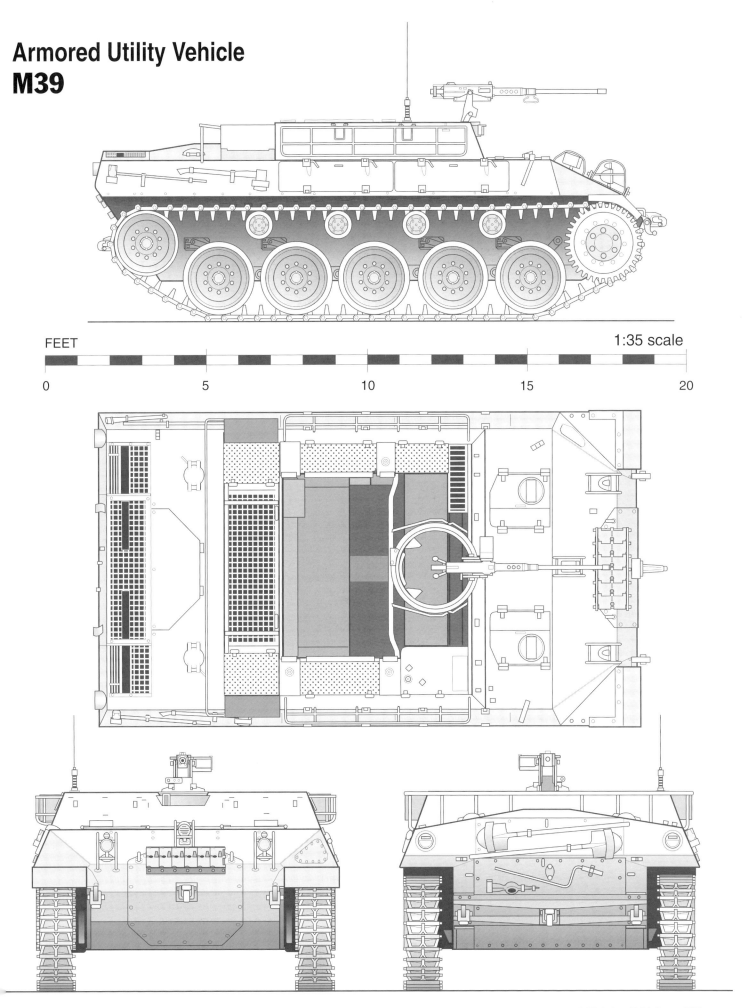

FEET

1:35 scale

0   5   10   15   20

The M39 armored utility vehicle evolved from the T41 and went into production in late 1944
as a towing vehicle for the 90mm gun T15 and the 3 inch gun carriage M6.

M24 Light Tank
Chaffee

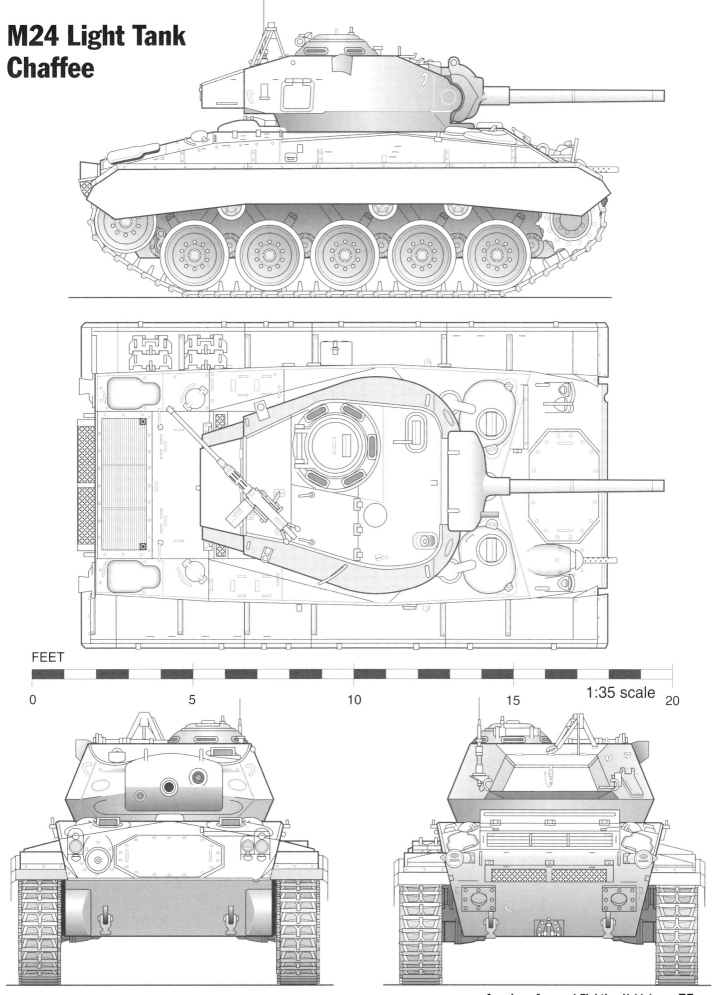

FEET

0   5   10   15   1:35 scale   20

LVT(A)-1 Landing Vehicle Tracked (Armored) Mk. 1

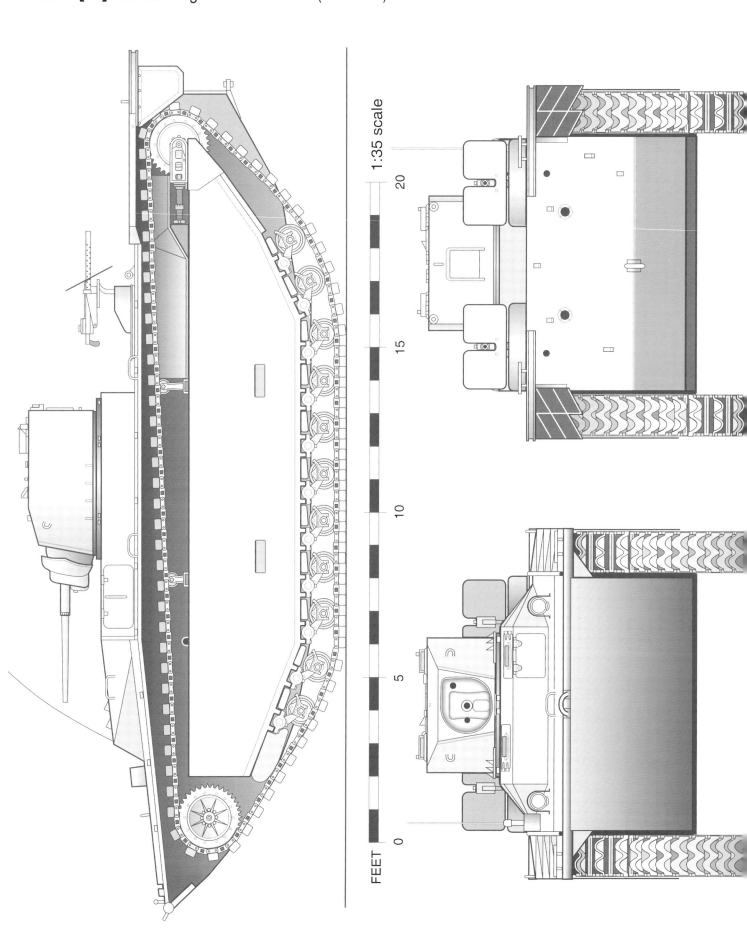

1:35 scale

FEET

0 5 10 15 20

LVT(A)-1 Landing Vehicle Tracked (Armored) Mk. 1

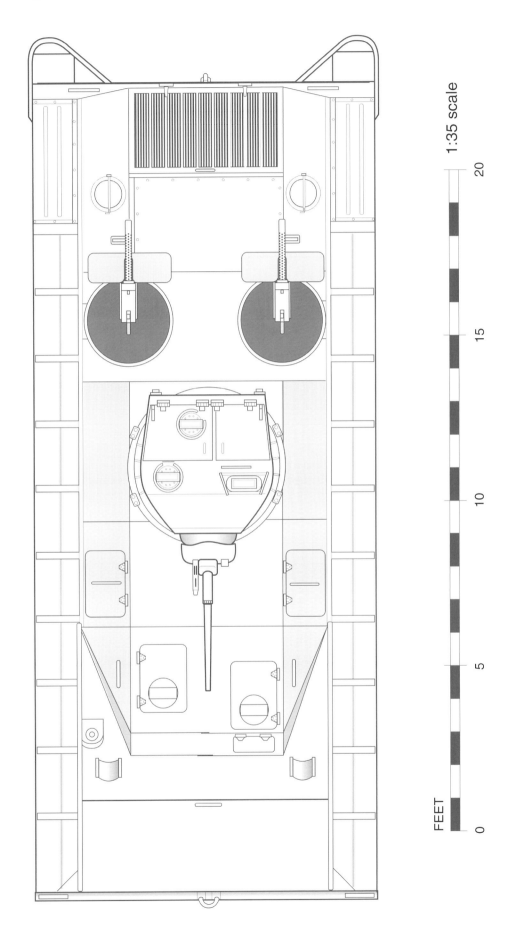

1:35 scale

FEET

0 5 10 15 20

Light Tank M22 (T9E1) Locust

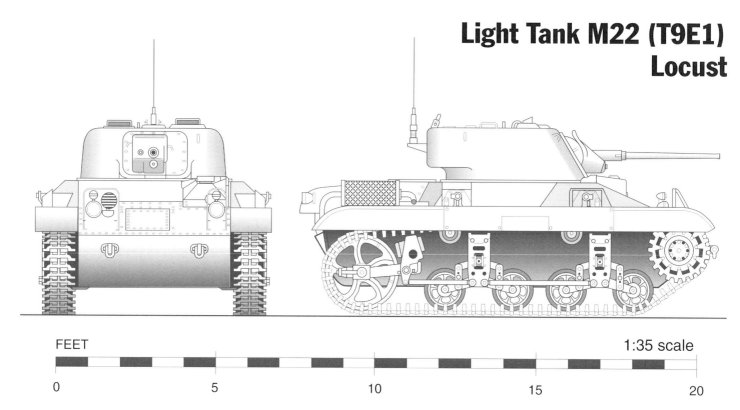

FEET   1:35 scale

0   5   10   15   20

The requirement for an airborne light tank had been seeded in the USA well before they entered WW2. Plans were submitted in mid-1941 and acceptance was given to the Marmon-Herrington design. The weight limit target was set at 7.5 tons, but by the time the first T9 prototype appeared it was obvious that 8 tons was more realistic. By November 1942 the first T9E1 was sent to APG for testing, and a second one was sent to Britain. Even before these tests were completed, quantity production for 500 vehicles was approved. Serious production began in April 1943 and continued until February 1944 for a total production of 830 vehicles, now standardized as the M22. The truth is that these little tanks, named "Locust" by the British, never did see service with the American Forces. However, a few intermingled with Tetrarchs saw service with the British 6th Airborne in the Rhine crossing of March 24, 1945. By July 1945 the M22 was declared as obsolete.

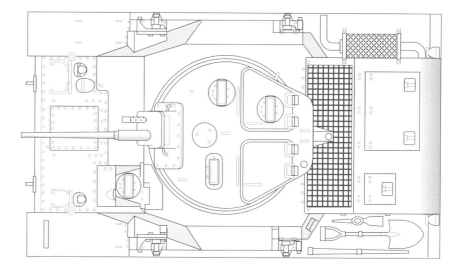

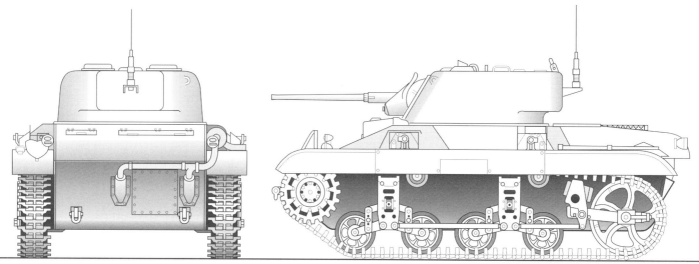

T1E3 Aunt Jemima
Mine Exploder

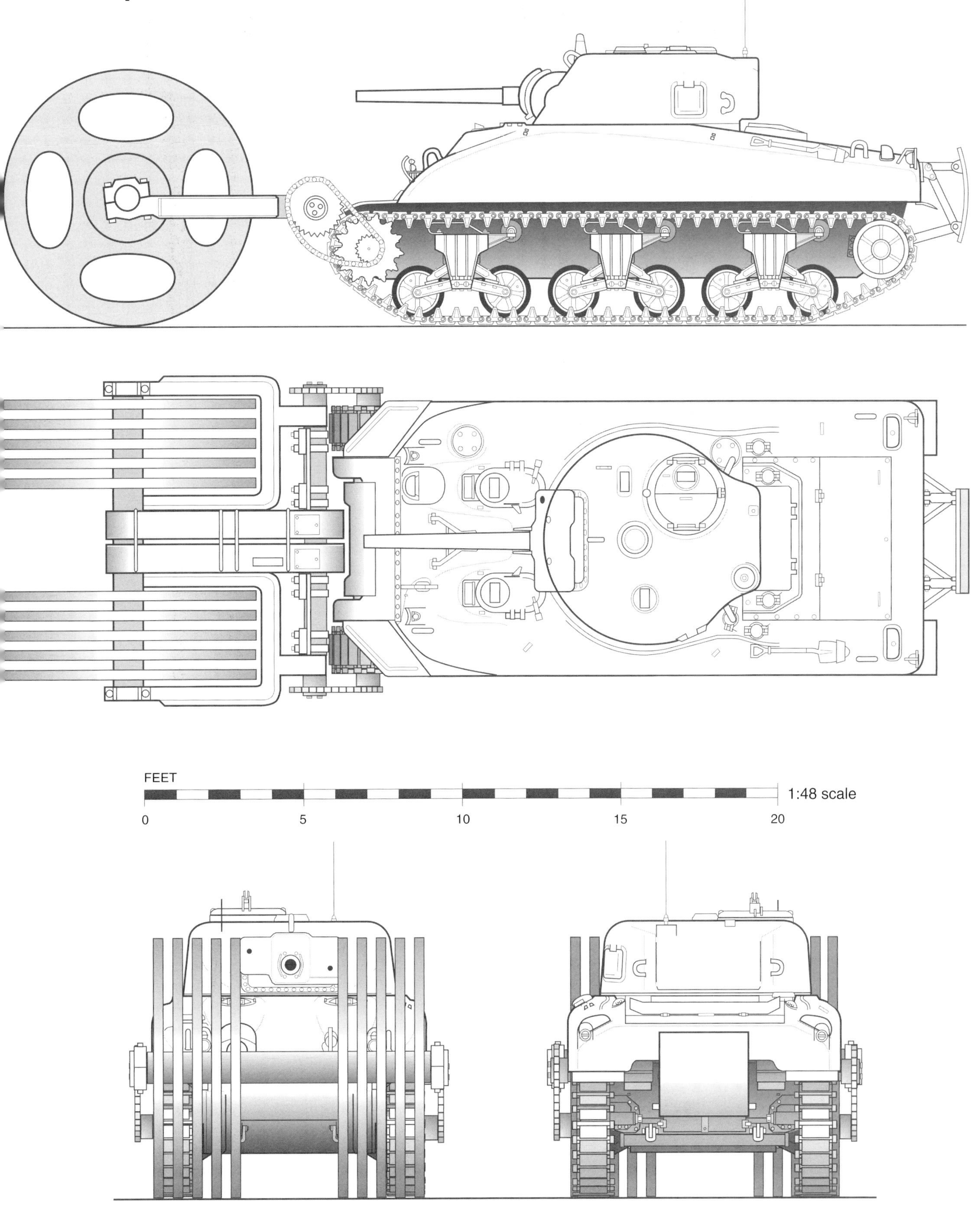

FEET

0   5   10   15   20

1:48 scale

LVT(A)-4 early
Landing Vehicle Tracked (Armored) Mk. 4

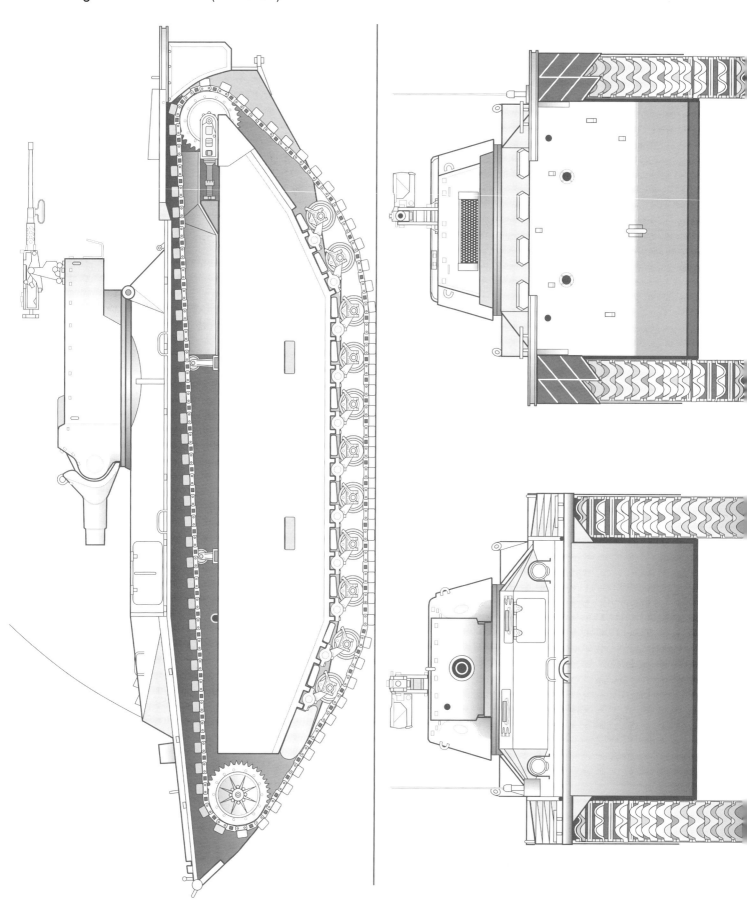

LVT(A)-4 early
Landing Vehicle Tracked (Armored) Mk. 4

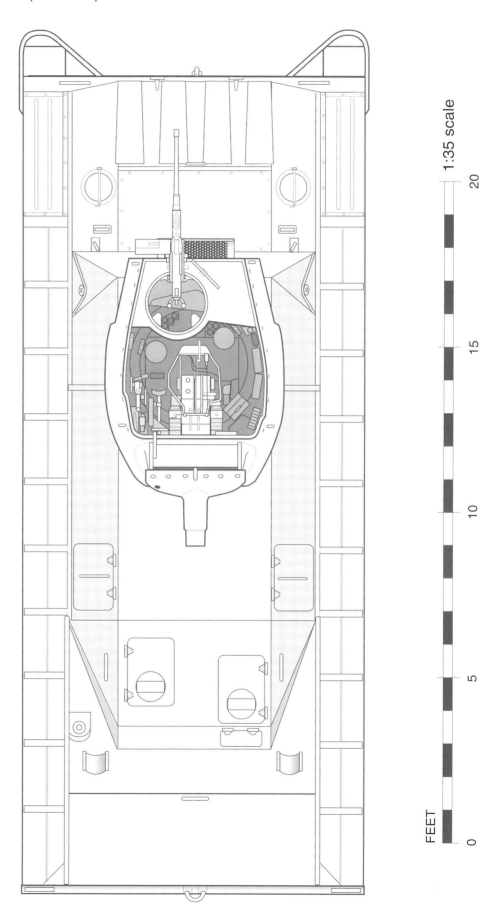

1:35 scale

FEET

0   5   10   15   20

M36 90mm Gun Motor Carriage

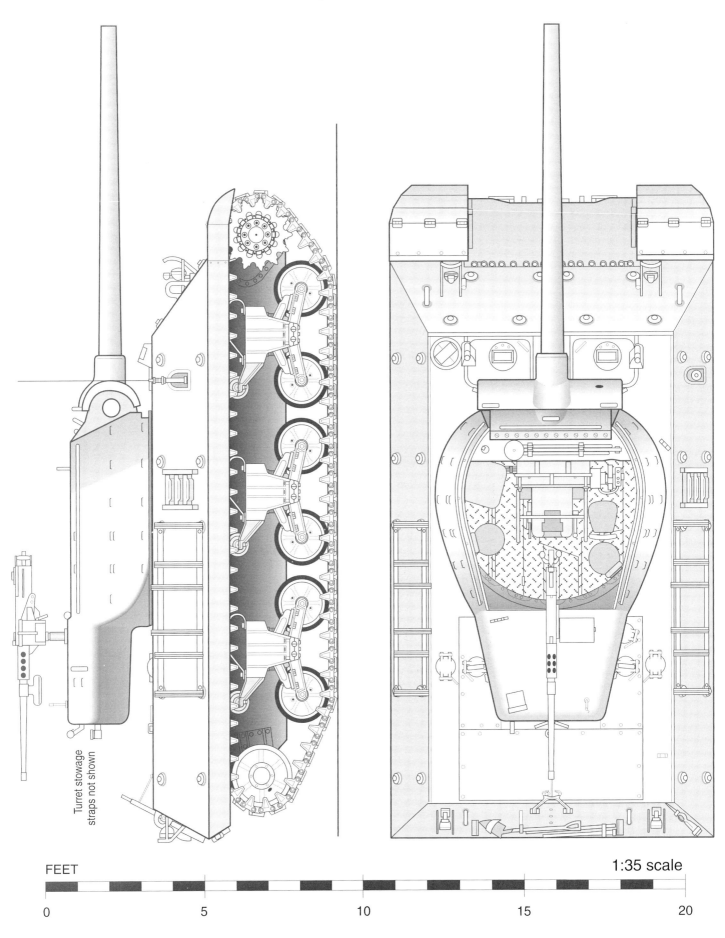

Turret stowage straps not shown

FEET

1:35 scale

0   5   10   15   20

M36 90mm Gun Motor Carriage

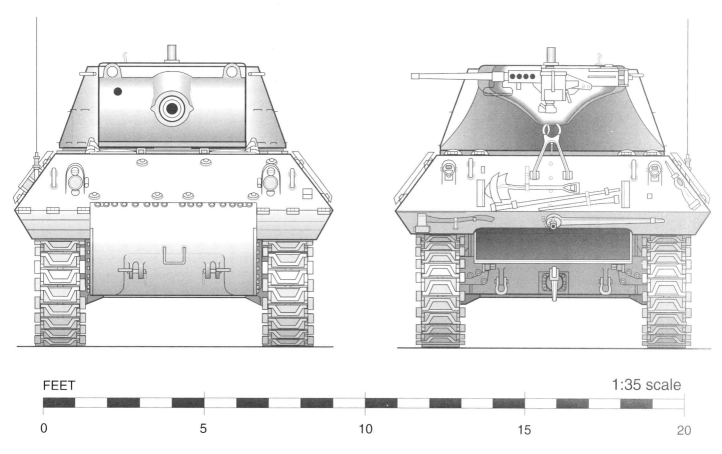

FEET

1:35 scale

0   5   10   15   20

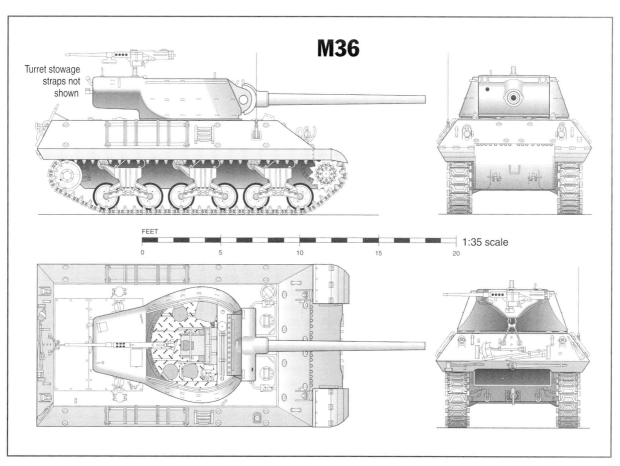

M36

Turret stowage straps not shown

FEET

1:35 scale

0   5   10   15   20

M36B1 90mm Gun Motor Carriage

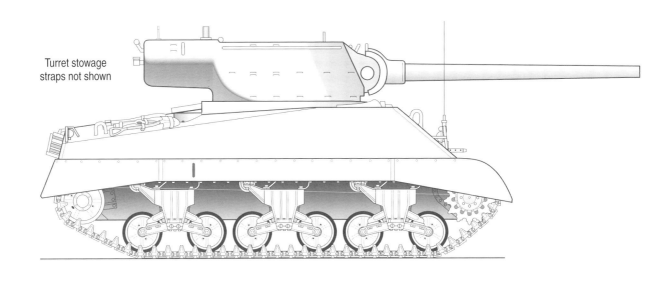

Turret stowage
straps not shown

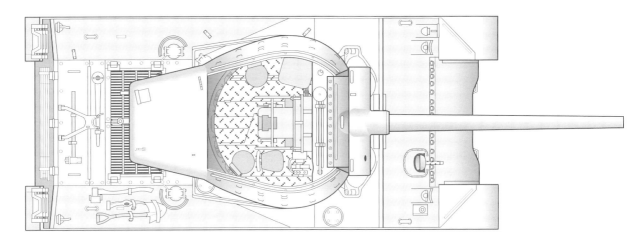

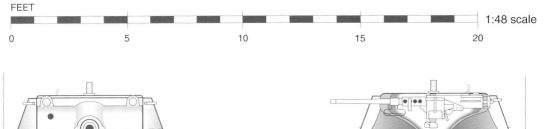

FEET

0   5   10   15   20

1:48 scale

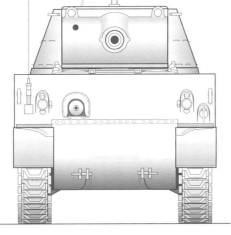

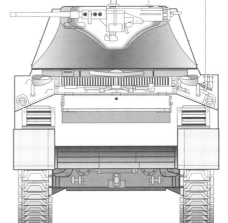

105mm Howitzer Motor Carriage **M37**

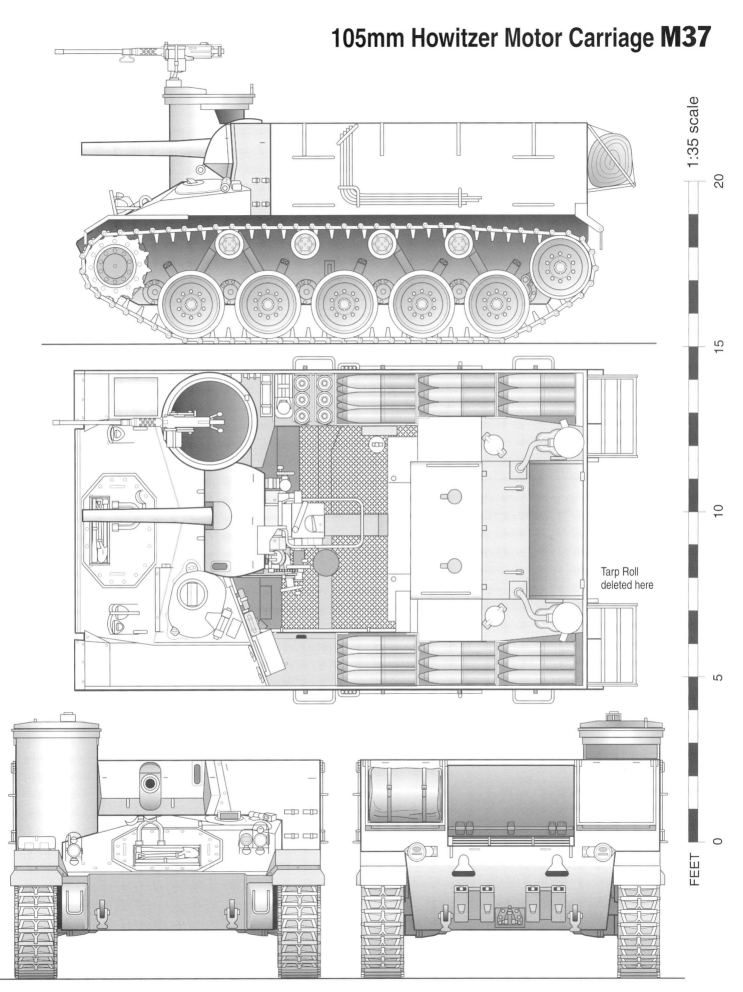

1:35 scale

Tarp Roll
deleted here

20

15

10

5

0

FEET

Sherman "Calliope"
T34 Rocket Launcher

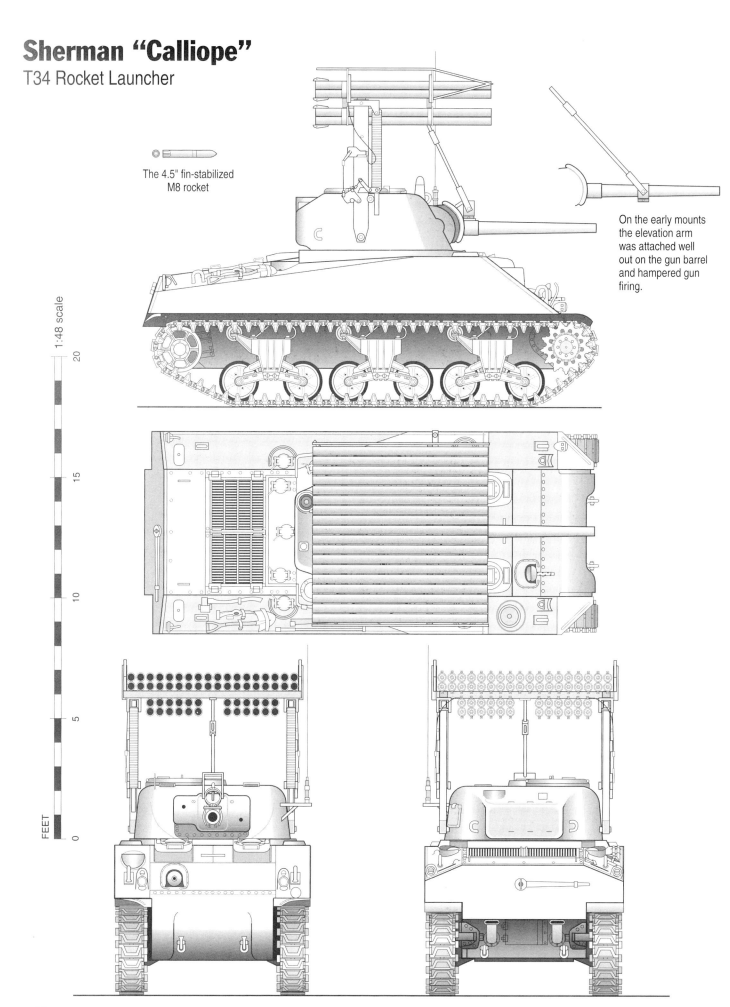

The 4.5" fin-stabilized
M8 rocket

On the early mounts
the elevation arm
was attached well
out on the gun barrel
and hampered gun
firing.

1:48 scale

20

15

10

5

FEET

0

GMC DUKW-353
Initial production model

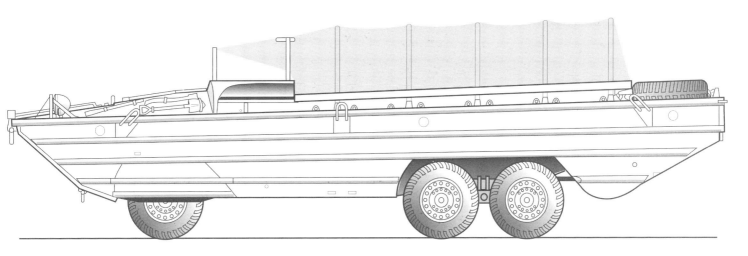

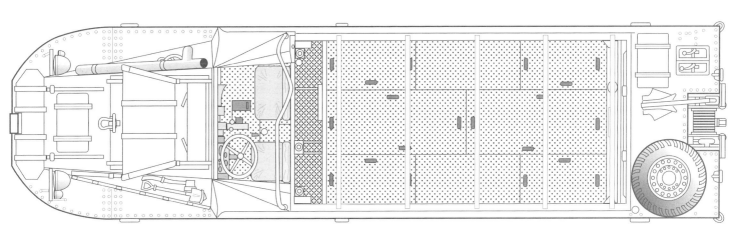

FEET

0   5   10   15   20

1:48 scale

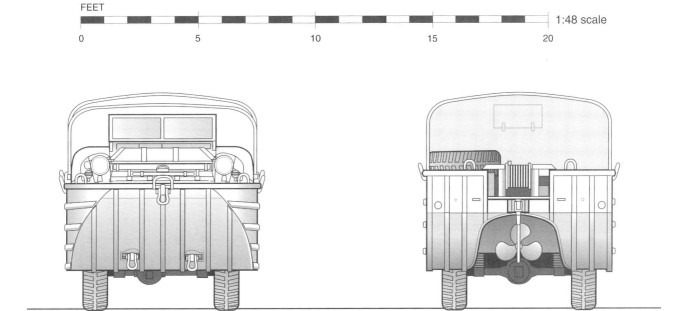

M4A3(76)W HVSS
(Often referred to as M4A3E8)

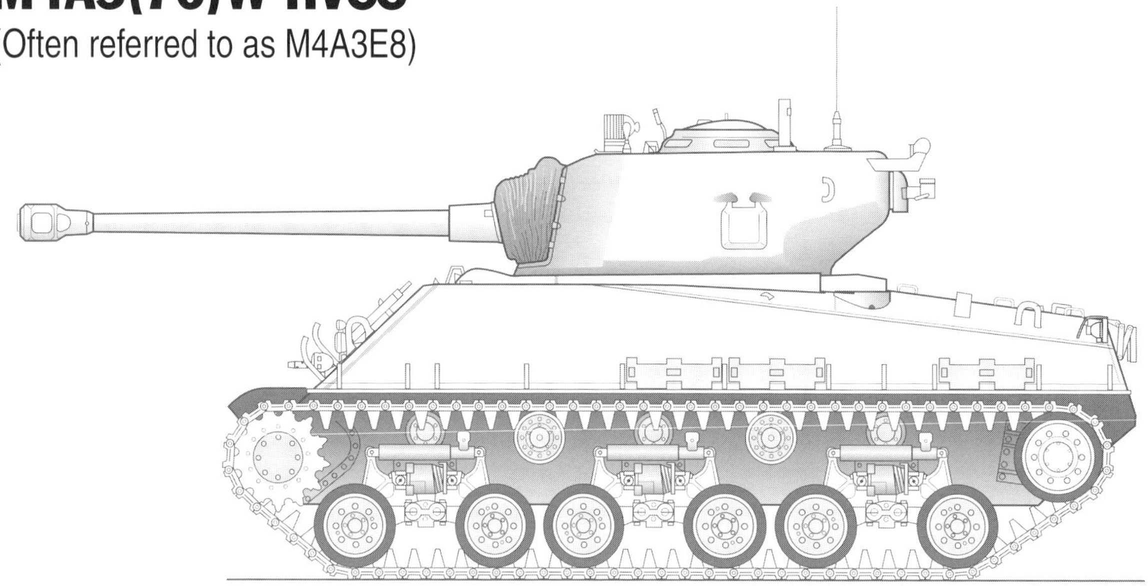

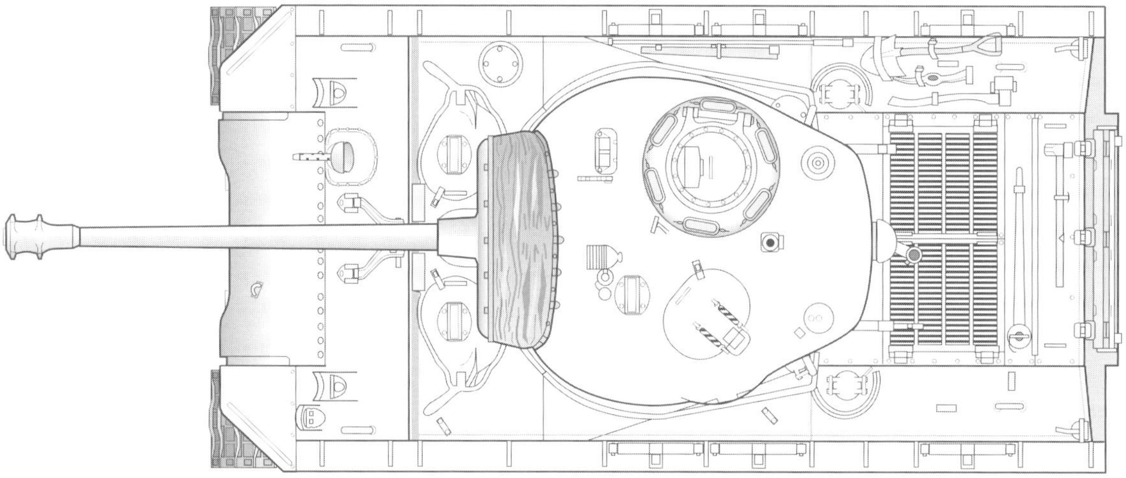

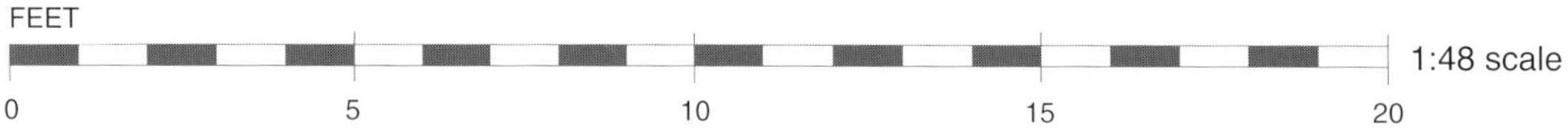

FEET

0   5   10   15   20

1:48 scale

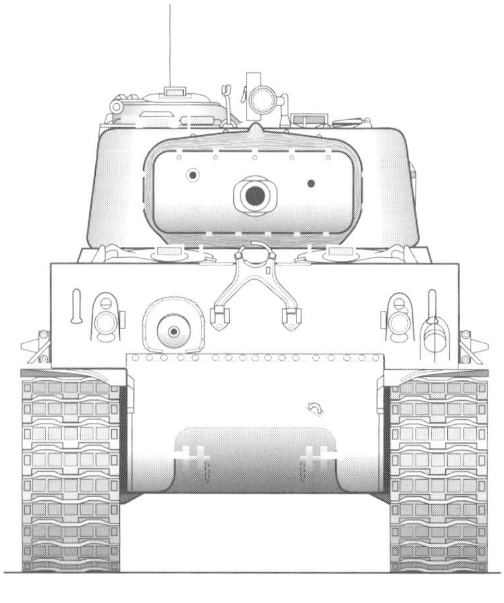

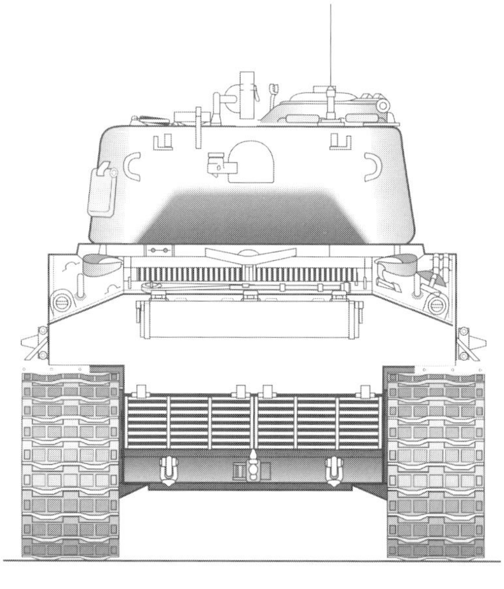

T26 Pershing
Heavy Tank

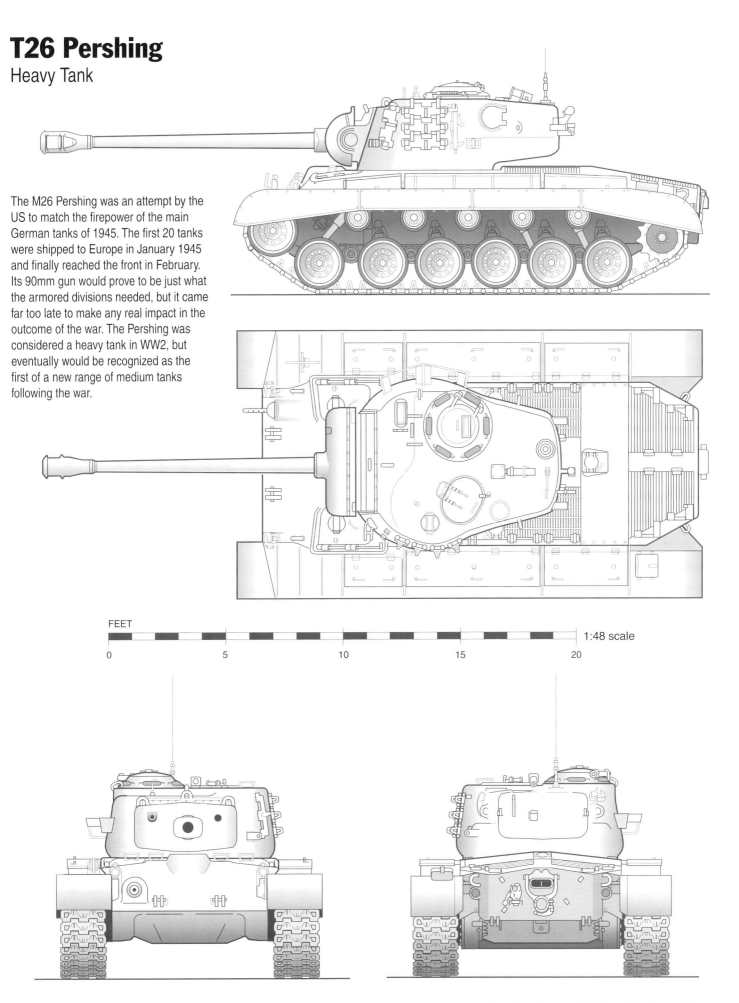

The M26 Pershing was an attempt by the US to match the firepower of the main German tanks of 1945. The first 20 tanks were shipped to Europe in January 1945 and finally reached the front in February. Its 90mm gun would prove to be just what the armored divisions needed, but it came far too late to make any real impact in the outcome of the war. The Pershing was considered a heavy tank in WW2, but eventually would be recognized as the first of a new range of medium tanks following the war.

FEET

0   5   10   15   20

1:48 scale

T26E4 Super Pershing

Temporary Pilot No. 1, Europe, April 1945
3rd Armored Division

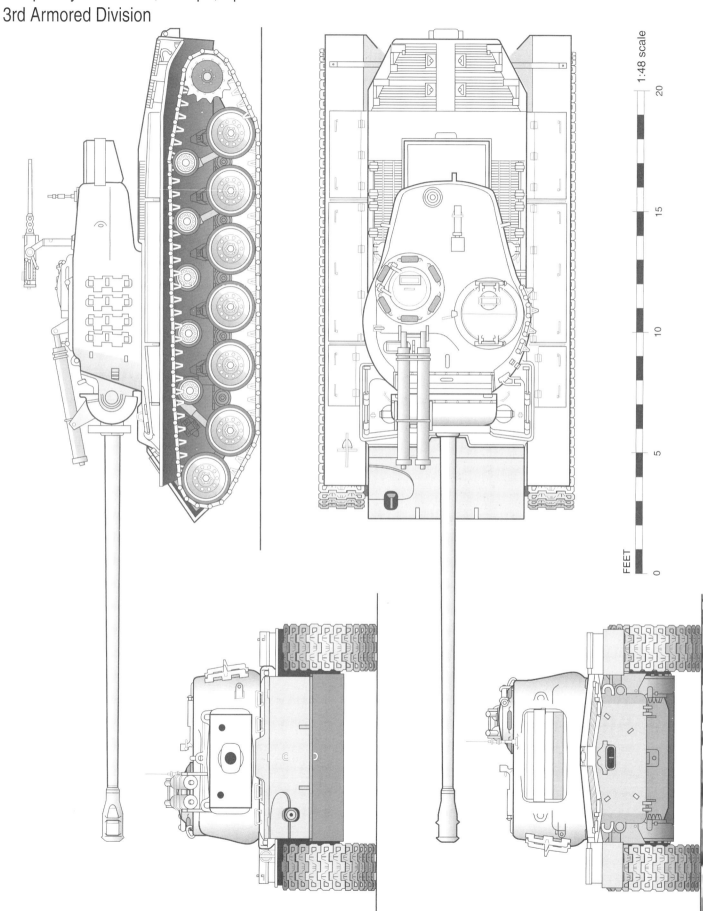

1:48 scale

Superheavy Tank T28
(105mm Gun Motor Carriage T95)

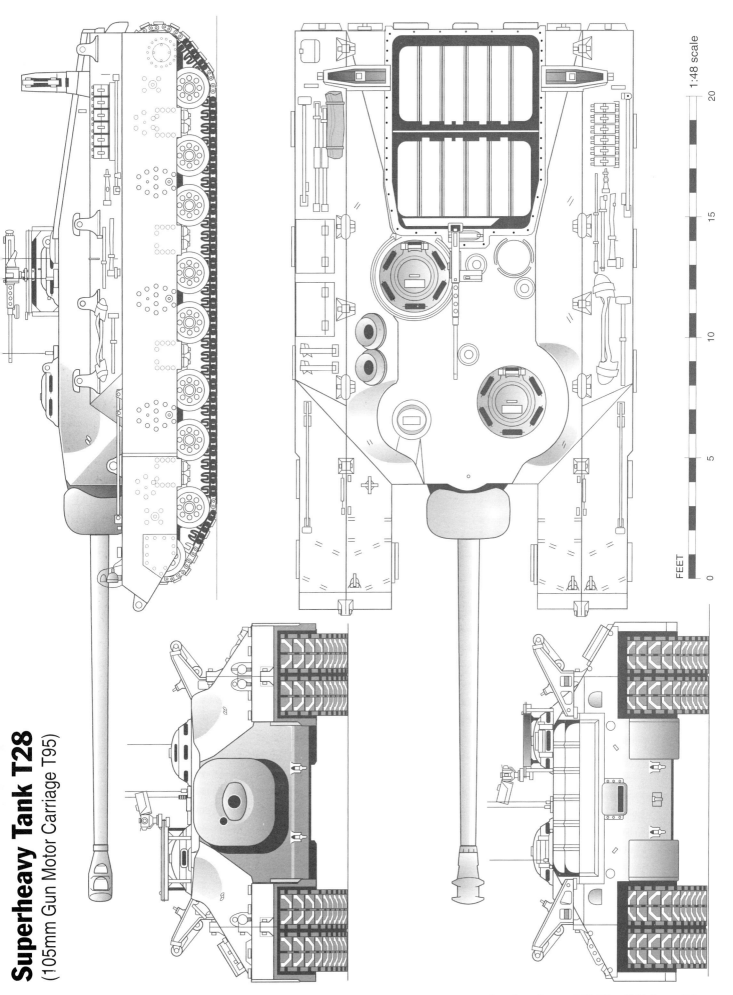

1:48 scale

FEET

0   5   10   15   20

This interesting ACME Newspicture, Washington Bureau photo was taken at Aberdeen Proving Ground in October 1946 when the T28 went on display at the 28th Annual Meeting of the Army Ordnance Association. The T28 was a late war development of a superheavy assault tank intended for use during the final push into Germany. It had 12" frontal armor, a 105mm gun and weighed in at 90 tons. An order for five units was placed but only two were built before the war ended and production ceased.

Bibliography

Chamberlain, P., and C. Ellis. *British and American Tanks of World War II*. London: Arms and Armour Press, 1969.

Crowe, D., and R.J. Icks. *Encyclopedia of Armoured Cars*. Secaucus, NJ: Chartwell Books Inc., 1976.

———. *Encyclopedia of Tanks*. London: Barry & Jenkins Limited, 1975.

Fletcher, D. *Tanks in Camera, 1940–1943*. Stroud, UK: Sutton Publishing Limited, 1998.

Forty, G. *A Photo History of Armoured Cars in Two World Wars*. Poole, UK: Blandford Press, 1984.

———. *United States Tanks of World War II*. Poole, UK: Blandford Press, 1983.

Green, M. *M4 SHERMAN: Combat and Development History of the Sherman Tank and All Sherman Variants*. Osceola, WI: Motorbooks International, 1993.

Halberstadt, H. *Inside the Great Tanks*. London: Windrow & Greene Ltd., 1997.

Harlem, P. *Modeler's Guide to the Sherman*. Del Ray, FL: Ampersand Publishing, 1998.

Hunnicutt, R. P. *ARMORED CAR: A History of American Wheeled Combat Vehicles*. Novato, CA: Presidio Press, 2002.

———. *BRADLEY: A History of American Fighting and Support Vehicles*. Novato, CA: Presidio Press, 1999.

———. *FIREPOWER: A History of the American Heavy Tank*. Novato, CA: Presidio Press, 1988.

———. *HALF-TRACK: A History of American Semi-Tracked Vehicles*. Novato, CA: Presidio Press, 2001.

———. *PERSHING: A History of the Medium Tank T20 Series*. Berkeley, CA: Feist Publications, 1971.

———. *SHERMAN: A History of the American Medium Tank*. San Rafael, CA: Taurus Enterprises, 1978.

———. *STUART: A History of the American Light Tank*. Novato, CA: Presidio Press, 1992.

Icks, Robert J. *Tanks & Armored Vehicles, 1900–1945*. Old Greenwich, CT: WE Inc., 1967.

ISO Military Vehicle Series. *Studebaker M29 Weasel*, London: ISO Publications, 1985.

Kern, P. R. *The Studebaker M29 Weasel*. N.p.: Studebaker Corporation, n.d.

Lemons, C. *Organization and Markings of United States Armored Units, 1918–1941*. Atglen: Schiffer Publishing Ltd., 2004.

Macksey, K. *Rommel: Battles and Campaigns*. Toronto: Thomas Nelson & Sons Ltd., 1979.

Mesko, J. *M3 Half-Track in Action*. Carrollton, TX: Squadron/Signal Publications, n.d.

———. *M3 Lee/Grant in Action*. Carrollton, TX: Squadron/Signal Publications, 1995.

———. *U.S. Armored Cars in Action*. Carrollton, TX: Squadron/Signal Publications, 1995.

———. *U.S. Self-Propelled Guns in Action*. Carrollton, TX: Squadron/Signal Publications, 1999.

Perkins, N. H. & M.E. Rogers. *Roll Again Second Armored*. Surrey, UK: Kristall Productions Ltd., 1988.

Zaloga, S. J. *Stuart: U.S. Light Tanks in Action*. Carrollton, TX: Squadron/Signal Publications, 1979.

———. *Tank Battles of the Pacific War, 1941–1945*. Hong Kong: Concord Publications Co., 1995.

———. *U.S. Tank Destroyers in Combat, 1941–1945*. Hong Kong: Concord Publications Co., 1996.

Basic Tank Components

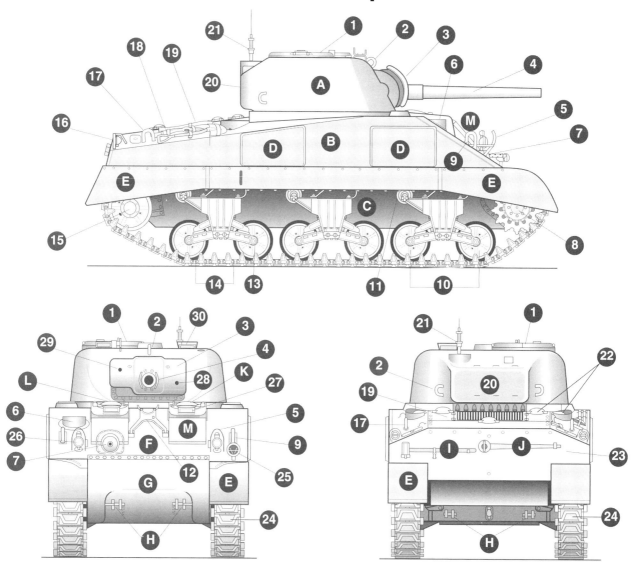

A. Cast Turret
B. Upper Hull
C. Lower Hull
D. Appliqué Armor
E. Dust Skirt
F. Glacis Plate
G. Transmission Housing
H. Towing Brackets
I. Sledge Hammer
J. Idler Adjusting Wrench
K. Driver's Hatch
L. Assist. Driver Hatch
M. Angled 1" Plate

1. Commander's Hatch
2. Turret Lift Hook
3. Gun Mantlet
4. Main Gun
5. Headlamp Guard
6. Ventilator
7. Bow Machinegun
8. Drive Sprocket
9. Hull Lift Hook
10. Bogie Suspension Unit
11. Trailing Return Roller
12. Gun Lock
13. Road Wheel
14. Track Links
15. Rear Idler Wheel

16. Tail Lights
17. Chassis Lift Hook
18. Tools
19. Engine Deck
20. Turret Bustle
21. Radio Aerial
22. Fuel Filler Caps
23. Rear Plate
24. Track Shoe
25. Siren
26. Driving Light
27. Driver's Periscope
28. Coaxial Machine Gun
29. Main Gun Sight
30. Loader's Periscope

VARIOUS MODELING SCALES

Scale	1 inch equals	1 scale foot =	1 scale meter =	Comments
1:4	4"	3"	250.0 mm	Flying Models, Live-steam Trains
1:8	8"	$1^1/_2$"	125.0 mm	Cars, Motorcycles, Trains
1:12	1'	1"	83.3 mm	Cars, Motorcycles, Dollhouses
1:16	1' 4"	$^3/_4$"	62.5 mm	Cars, Motorcycles, Trains
1:20	1' 8"	$^{19}/_{32}$"	50.0 mm	Cars
1:22.5	1' 10$^1/_2$"	$^{17}/_{32}$"	44.4 mm	G-Scale Trains
1:24	2'	$^1/_2$"	41.7 mm	Cars, Trucks, Dollhouses
1:25	2' 1"	$^{15}/_{32}$"	40.0 mm	Cars, Trucks
1:32	2' 8"	$^3/_8$"	31.25 mm	Aircraft, Cars, Tanks, Trains
1:35	2' 11"	$^{11}/_{32}$"	28.57 mm	Armor
1:43	3' 7"	$^9/_{32}$"	23.25 mm	Cars, Trucks
1:48	4'	$^1/_4$"	20.83 mm	Aircraft, Armor, O-Scale Trains
1:64	5' 4"	$^3/_{16}$"	15.62 mm	Aircraft, S-Scale Trains
1:72	6'	$^{11}/_{63}$"	13.88 mm	Aircraft, Armor, Boats
1:76	6' 4"	$^5/_{32}$"	13.16 mm	Armor
1:87	7' 3"	—	11.49 mm	Armor, HO-Scale Trains
1:96	8'	$^1/_8$"	10.42 mm	1/8" Scale Ships, Aircraft
1:100	8' 4"	—	10.00 mm	Aircraft
1:125	10' 5"	—	8.00 mm	Aircraft
1:144	12'	—	6.94 mm	Aircraft
1:160	13' 4"	—	6.25 mm	N-Scale Trains
1:192	16'	$^1/_{16}$"	5.21 mm	$^1/_{16}$" Scale Ships
1:200	16' 8"	—	5.00 mm	Aircraft, Ships

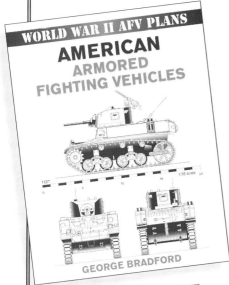